WORLD WAR I

in Outline

B. H. Liddell Hart

WESTHOLME
Yardley

Originally published by Faber & Faber in 1936.

Westholme Publishing, LLC
904 Edgewood Road
Yardley, Pennsylvania 19067
Visit our Web site at www.westholmepublishing.com

First Printing March 2012
10 9 8 7 6 5 4 3 2 1

ISBN: 978-1-59416-161-2

Printed in the United States of America.

PREFACE

This outline of the World War is a sequence of salient facts—beads on the thread of history. It is an attempt to let the facts tell the story, as plainly as possible, without the embroidery of criticism and argument. Comment, therefore, is limited to the emphasis occasionally needed to make clear the significance of a fact.

Selection, of course, is inevitable in compiling any record of facts. The guiding principle, here, has been to pick out those which definitely moulded the course of events. They comprise four kinds of fact: the explicit ideas which prompted any major move, the conditions in which this took place, the main data of the action which ensued, the ascertainable consequences. The last three are summarized wherever possible in the words of an authoritative record. The first is given wherever possible in the words, at the time, of the men responsible. This offers the least speculative course in tracing not only what happened, but why it happened. Also it is fairer that the performance of such leaders should be judged by what they said rather than by what others have said of them since, either in criticism or apology.

This outline, however, is primarily concerned with the course of events. It does not attempt to weigh men, but only such of their thoughts and actions as decisively influenced history. It may thus tend to give a better or worse impression of an individual than would appear in a just biographical balance. The reader should bear this in mind. It would be out of accord with the factual nature of this outline to introduce personal impressions. In dealing with the Somme or Passchendaele, for example, it would be historically irrelevant to insert a compensatory reference to Haig's military virtues. In his strength of purpose, his technical competence within the natural limits of his training, his balance of judgment where no preconception or prejudice affected the scales, it is probable that he was surpassed by few, if any, of his contemporaries. Yet the deeper one goes into the causation of events, the more difficult it is to find places where his qualities had a decisively advantageous effect on the situation, while it becomes only too clear where his misjudgments proved decisive for ill. In the scales of a biographer, even a critical biographer, his faults may be outweighed by his qualities; but in the scales of history they are preponderant. That condition proved general in the leadership of the war.

In part, it was the natural consequence of the conditions which bounded the exercise of high command in a war of masses. The remoteness of the higher commanders from the battlefield made it even more difficult for them to gauge the real situation there than it was for them to influence that situation. Whereas in Napoleon's time it had been true to say that the best general was the one who made the fewest mistakes, it was nearer the truth now that the best general was the one who caused the least mistakes. Actual command was split into a myriad fragments, resting in the hands of the company and platoon leaders: the higher commanders had changed into company directors. Deprived of personal experience of battlefield reality, they were handicapped in correcting the inevitable discrepancies of pre-war theory: in checking the theory with the facts, and in adjusting it to the new developments. Preconceptions and prejudices, personal and professional, were thus ridden on a loose rein—and easily ran away with the riders.

The latest edition of *Field Service Regulations* fittingly recognizes that high command in war requires:

The broadest possible outlook and knowledge, of social as well as of military questions. War is now more than ever a social problem: a major war affects the whole of the national life and every class of citizen, and there is a corresponding civil influence on the conduct of military operations.

It is significant to compare this with the admissions in the biography of Haig which was written by General Charteris, who was for so many years his intimate assistant:

He took little interest in politics. . . . He had strangely little learning; his military work absorbed him, and he only glanced at other subjects, never studied them . . . he read few books and never a single novel . . . it was a matter of constant wonder that events outside his immediate task could stir his interest so little. He had not a critical mind.

Field Service Regulations also emphasizes that:

Tactics on the battlefield are governed by certain simple common-sense precepts, which are in the main very similar to those which govern everyday life. The ordinary citizen who is planning a business transaction goes through much the same steps as the commander in the field who is planning an operation. . . . Both have to take into their calculations the possible schemes of rivals.

and the main contrast is:

not that the common-sense qualities required in war are different from those required in peace but that the conditions of war are utterly unfamiliar to the ordinary civilized man.

While the professional soldier in peace-time has as little opportunity as the ordinary citizen to become familiar with the stresses of battle, he becomes so habituated to military processes that he can perform them instinctively in the heat of action, so that his functional efficiency is apt to be less affected by the "friction" of war. Here lies his advantage. But it applies in far less degree to the higher sphere of war, where it may be outweighed by handicaps that are inevitable in peacetime soldiering. The politician is always "at war," the business man in competition with others. They have constant practice in conflict, and unceasing experience of its psychological conditions. Soldiering, by contrast, is a sheltered occupation save in war. The higher a man rises in the profession the less is he called on to contend with opposition, and the more immune he becomes even from criticism. The ease with which the will of the superior prevails inside an army becomes a handicap in preparation for dealing with a hostile army. Always revolving between the poles of authority and obedience, the soldier gains little or no psychological experience as a fighter. His training tends to suppress rather than to develop the combative qualities. Exercises in mimic war, regulated by umpires, cannot compare with the exacting tests of the political or the business field.

An appreciation of these conditions may arouse sympathy for the generals of the World War, who from the isolation of a headquarters office, had to direct armies of millions composed of the people in arms, and were pitted against an active foe in a warfare which embraced a diversity of factors that were military only by adoption. There is no cause for surprise that they failed so often to gauge their steps, or the enemy's; rather is it remarkable, when all is weighed, that they adapted themselves even as well as they did to conditions for which they were, by training and environment, so little prepared.

Yet this reflection leads to another—on the way that square pegs were placed in round holes. Although it was a war of nations, and many of the best brains of the nation were drawn into the forces, they were excluded from those military spheres in which "the broadest possible outlook and knowledge" were needed. The custom of all the armies erected the principle that no one was fit to have a voice in matters of strategy unless he had nearly forty years' practice of military routine. It was certainly a novel principle, since it would have excluded nearly all the great commanders of history—from Alexander, Hannibal and Cæsar, down to Cromwell, Marlborough and Napoleon. And it was the more strange since the twentieth century strategist had to deal with many more non-military factors. But although the principle flew in the face of historical experience and modern knowledge, it was rigidly maintained—except in the Dominion forces—throughout the four years of war.

By a practical paradox, the civilian was invited to take over the most strictly professional functions of soldiering while he was viewed as an intruder in the higher and hence less technical posts. Any intelligent civilian with administrative experience found it easy to master the details of staff-work—as soon as he had ·"learnt the language" his past experience here became ·a strong asset. In comparison, it was far more difficult for him to become an efficient regimental officer. Proficiency in the operative technique of an infantry or artillery unit, in a regular army, is the product of habit as well as of specialized training. On the other hand, given normal intelligence, it does not take long to acquire the broad knowledge of artillery tactics that a general from the infantry or cavalry, or of infantry tactics that a general from the artillery, is likely to have. It is also worth emphasis that the decisions which an army commander had to take in the last war, though great in responsibility, were simple in their technical elements compared with those of a battalion commander. If a layman had attended a conference of army commanders he would have been able to follow the discussion with far more understanding than if he had been present at a conference of company or battery commanders. The one dealt largely in generalities, the other in technicalities. Generals need to be truly general in their knowledge and understanding. Otherwise the best professional soldier may be no more than an amateur of war.

The higher the plane of war, the more the solution of its problems depends on wide knowledge, broad out-look, and depth of thought: and the less, comparative-ly, on technical experience. This does not mean that knowledge of military technique is unnecessary: with-out it, the ablest man would be handicapped, especial-ly in dealing with forces which have a long-established system of operation. The principles of fighting are based on common sense, but something more is needed to apply them effectively in the handling of armies. The better a man's mental equipment, however, the less time he will take to acquire an adequate knowl-edge of such technique. And in acquiring it quickly he will have an advantage over the man who has taken thirty or forty years in climbing the military ladder. He will have little to unlearn, his knowledge will be fresh, and he will have had an actual operative experi-ence of the latest instruments and methods. These will have changed, and often be entirely new, since the oth-er man served his apprenticeship to arms. It is difficult for the older soldier to have a sure grasp of weapons he has never handled, and of methods he has never carried out. Moreover, if his technical experience lies several steps back, it becomes still more difficult for him to gauge the next step forward. What he gains by having prolonged experience of command may be offset by lacking first-hand knowledge of the present tools of command.

Another asset for high command is personal experience of fighting and the effects of fire. For what is tactically impossible cannot be strategically sound. To know "what can't be done" is the beginning of military wisdom—and the best incentive to discover what can be done. The British Army began the war with an advantage over the others in this qualification, for many of the generals had gained such personal experience in South Africa. But before long it lapsed, because the conditions of fighting and the effects of fire developed so vastly, while the higher command receded so far from the fighting line—from contact with reality. Thus there was yet another asset which could only be possessed by the man who climbed the ladder rapidly.

That opportunity was only vouchsafed in the Dominion Forces. Its results are significant. Since technical proficiency and executive habit count for more in the lower grades, it is to be inferred that a non-professional soldier who proved himself barely the equal of many regulars as a battalion or brigade commander might prove outstanding when, and if, he reached a higher command. That inference was confirmed by actual experience in the Dominion Forces.

When the conditions of the War are analyzed, it becomes clear that in the qualifications for high command, and still more for strategic direction, there was little in pre-war professional experience that helped a man, while there was much that might handicap the development of his personal qualities. An objective study of the past would have been a guide to the conditions that were in development, but for such study professional soldiers had no training and limited opportunity. The discovery of uncomfortable facts had never been encouraged in armies, who treated their history as a sentimental treasure rather than a field of scientific research. Thus all were amateurs in that war from the moment when the opening moves broke down, and the real nature of the war emerged from the artificial mould of convention in which the pre-war plans and forces had been cast. The question which remained was how quickly they could learn, and whether their minds could expand to the scale of the problems. The chances of this adaptation, as well as the opportunity for fresh minds, were diminished by a delusion—that they were professionals in the larger sphere. This was the "Great Delusion" of the "Great War."

Its direct consequences can be measured by comparing the record of their assumptions with the run of the facts. Its indirect consequences are immeasurable.

CONTENTS

MAPS

PROLOGUE

To show how the World War arose it would be necessary to trace the conflict of national aims and the course of international "incidents" for at least half a century before 1914. Yet this would only be a study of the causes near the surface. The deeper currents, as from time immemorial, were those of lower human nature—possessiveness, competitiveness, vanity. When men talked of nations they personified them, and that personification took a form which was worse than the sum of the individuals composing them. The nation was represented by the lowest common denominator.

More than two thousand years had passed since Plato reached the conclusion: "Until either the philosophers are the rulers or the men who are now called kings and potentates become genuine and adequate philosophers there can be no respite from evil for the states, nor, I think, for the whole human race." Twenty-four centuries of further experience had brought no such change in the ways of rulership nor shown reason to change that conclusion. Whatever the system of government it was inseparable from the desire to govern men—as opposed to the philosophical desire to discover the truth and share its light, so that other men may find their own way.

Many of those who exercised power had much that was good in them. Few were without some good in them. But none were wholly free from the lust of power. To keep their power it was easier, and seemed, safer, to appeal to the lowest common denominator—to instinct rather than to reason, to interest rather than to right, to expediency rather than to principle. It sounded practical, and thus commanded respect where to speak of ideals would only stir up distrust. But in practice there is nothing more difficult than to discover where expediency lies—it is apt to lead from one expedient to another, in a vicious circle through endless knots. Good intentions are common in that pursuit, but merely pave the way into a hellish tangle. So it proved in the years that led to 1914.

THE SPARK AND THE POWDER

1. THE SPARK

On the morning of June 28th, 1914, the Archduke Franz Ferdinand was shot in the streets of obscure Serajevo by a young Slav nationalist. The assassin was the romantically emotional tool of a secret society of Serbian officers known as the "Black Hand." The Archduke died at eleven o'clock.

So far as his dim lights allowed he was, and had dreamed of proving himself, the friend of the Slavs who had murdered him. His death was most welcome to the ruling body of Austrian officialdom. It gave them the opportunity of executing their own designs under the excuse of avenging the man whose accession to the throne they had feared. By crushing Serbia they hoped to cement the Austrian empire against the Slav movement within its borders, while establishing its ascendency in the Balkans. And in consolidating the empire each member of the ruling body had the hope of consolidating his own position.

At eleven o'clock on July 28th Austria declared war on Serbia, opening a war which engulfed all the great and most of the small peoples of the world.

In 1878 Austria had occupied the Turkish provinces of Bosnia and Herzegovina: she had never fulfilled her promise to evacuate them after restoring order and prosperity. In 1908 the "Young Turk" revolution gave her an urge and an opportunity to convert her administration into a definite annexation. In taking this step so precipitately Aehrenthal, the Austrian Foreign Minister, broke faith with Russia, with whom he had been negotiating. The effect was made worse by Germany's peremptory demand that Russia should accept it under pain of a combined Austrian and German attack.

In 1912 Bulgaria, Serbia and Greece combined in an attack on Turkey, encouraged by the Russian Foreign Minister who saw in it a means to score a point against Austria and re-establish Russian prestige in the Balkans. Austria prepared to fight, her annoyance increased by alarm at the prospect of Serbia's aggrandizement. Germany gave her assurances of unflinching support. The imminent danger of the Balkan War spreading into a general European war was allayed by Britain's moderating influence and Germany's eventual co-operation with Britain.

The passing of this danger gave Sir Edward Grey, the British Foreign Minister, a happy feeling that further crises might be as peacefully settled. If he had been more willing to look beneath the surface he might have felt more concern. A compromise had been reached by relaxations of attitude too curious to be attributed, save by the guileless or the militarily ignorant, to a sincere desire for peace. The British Government failed to appreciate the extent to which foreign policy abroad was swayed by military calculations.

The Governments of Austria and Russia had now

reached a point when both, next time, would choose to fight rather than risk a loss of prestige. Official relations might be easier, but public animosity was spreading, to reinforce the military party in overcoming the caution of diplomacy.

The British ambassador in Vienna predicted that "the next time a Serbian crisis arises . . . I feel certain that Austria-Hungary will refuse to admit of any Russian interference in the dispute, and that she will proceed to settle the differences with her little neighbour, *coûte que coûte*." The Foreign Office regarded him as unduly pessimistic, although the ambassador in St. Petersburg gave a similar account of the tide of feelings in Russia. The ambassador in Berlin warned them of the strength of the military party there, especially "in the immediate entourage of the Emperor." Colonel House, the confidant of the American President, left Berlin early in June, 1914 with the conviction that the military party was determined on war, at the earliest opportunity, and would force the Kaiser's abdication if he opposed their desire. "It is militarism run stark mad," he wrote to President Wilson. In Austria the return of Conrad von Hötzendorf to the control of the army threw fresh weight into the scales of war.

A further weight was added by thoughts which were fathered by wishes. In Vienna, officialdom was "firmly convinced" that Russian Poland would rise in revolt as soon as the Austrian army had crossed the frontier. The Tsar and his counsellors likewise persuaded themselves that in a short time Austria would begin to break up internally. If these predictions proved to be delusions, each Government was sufficiently uneasy over its own internal state to see war as the safety-valve for mounting pressures.

The trail being laid, the spark was struck by the fatal shot at Serajevo, the Bosnian capital. The next day Berchtold, the successor to Aehrenthal's office and to the tradition of diplomatic deceit, declared to Conrad that the time had come to settle with Serbia once for all. Conrad was delighted at this response to his repeated promptings. These directors of policy were not affected by the report of their own police investigation that there were "no proofs of the Serbian Government's complicity" in the assassination.

On July 5th the Kaiser sent word that Austria "could depend on the complete support of Germany" in the event of war against Russia. A further impetus was given by the assurance that Russia's forces were "in no way ready for war"—and that Germany's were.

But Berchtold spent some time in drafting an ultimatum that would be suitable—on the 10th he told the German ambassador that he was still considering "what demands could be put that it would be wholly impossible for Serbia to accept." The delay allowed both countries to take preparatory military measures. And the German steamship companies were warned that they must be ready for "swift developments" when the Austrian note was presented. It is significant that the Berlin banks had been ordered "with special emphasis" to increase the cover of their foreign securities ten days before the Archduke's murder.

The ultimatum was delivered to Serbia on the 23rd, when the Prime Minister was away—and when the French President had left St. Petersburg by sea after paying a state visit to the Tsar. Only forty-eight hours were allowed for Serbia's acceptance of the drastic terms. It was followed up by a warning against "any interference" which Germany delivered to Russia, France and Britain.

France at once assured Russia of her support, but Sir Edward Grey declined to commit Britain. Instead he made proposals for joint mediation. Accepted by France and Italy they were rebuffed by Germany, the Kaiser describing them as "a tremendous piece of British insolence." He remarked that he was not going to follow Grey in prescribing to the Austrian Emperor "how to preserve his honour."

Meantime Serbia had managed to deliver her answer two minutes before the time expired. While the Austrian ambassador was bringing it back to Vienna, orders were sent out for the mobilization of the Austrian forces against Serbia. But the Serbian Government had yielded so far that the Kaiser, when he read their reply on the 28th, admitted that "every reason for war drops away"—although as a "satisfaction of honour" he considered that Austria should occupy the Serbian capital. He was satisfied that the mere shaking of the mailed fist had sufficed. The Chancellor, Bethmann-Hollweg, now sent a series of restraining notes to Vienna. Their effect was nullified by the inflammatory messages which the German General Staff was sending to the Austrian, telling them to "decline the advances of Britain in the interest of peace. A European war is the last chance of saving Austria-Hungary. Germany is ready to back Austria unreservedly."

The Austrian Government had already gone too far to draw back without loss of pride. For at the first sign of a change in the German attitude, Berchtold cynically said: "I think that a further attempt by the Entente Powers to bring about a peaceful solution remains possible only so long as a new situation has not been created by the declaration of war." To overcome the aged Emperor's doubts, he told him that the Serbians had already fired on Austrian troops: having obtained the Emperor's signature to the declaration of war, in which this fictitious justification was inserted, he deleted this particular statement before sending out the document.

The news of Austria's declaration of war on Serbia loosened the Russian Foreign Minister's restraining hand on the Russian General Staff. They insisted on the mobilization of their forces. When he suggested that this should be confined to the Austrian frontier, they argued that for "technical reasons" this was impracticable. He still hesitated. But after his pride had been stung by a warning next day from the German ambassador that "mobilization means war," he stiffened—and yielded, instead, to his own generals' demand for general mobilization. But the Tsar momentarily intervened. After receiving a conciliatory telegram from the Kaiser, who was now beginning to wilt at the prospect of actual war, he insisted on the night of the 29th that the order should be cancelled and a partial mobilization substituted.

Next morning the generals returned to the charge, declaring that this would "dislocate" the organization of the army.

Then, curiously, at midday on the 30th an important Berlin newspaper published a special edition announcing that Germany's mobilization had been ordered. The statement was soon contradicted, but it had a convenient effect for those who wanted war. For at six p.m., before the contradiction arrived, the Tsar gave way to his generals and passed the order for general mobilization. It was posted up next morning, and was followed a few hours later by the Austrian order. Germany's mobilization was not publicly proclaimed until the following day, but troop movements and other steps had already begun.

On the 31st, Germany had sent an ultimatum to Russia and also to France. Russia "must suspend every war measure" within twelve hours; France must say whether she would remain neutral "in a Russo-German war," and was told "mobilization will inevitably mean war." The Russian Foreign Minister replied that it was technically impossible to stop mobilization, but that so long as negotiations continued Russia would abstain from attack. But nothing else than complete surrender, an impossible expectation, would satisfy Germany.

The German General Staff had insisted that "the unusually favourable moment should be used to strike." So on August 1st the German ambassador duly delivered the declaration of war, which his Government had already sent without waiting for the Russian reply. The declaration of war on France was delayed until the 3rd, much to the disgust of the Chief of the General Staff, in the hope of securing Britain's neutrality. Chancellor Bethmann-Hollweg had already tried to bargain for this by a suggestion that, in return, Germany would not annex any part of France, apart from her colonies. While rejecting such tenders the British Government was still undecided, and divided, as to action in support of France.

But on August 2nd, Germany, in fulfillment of her long-prepared war-plan, delivered an ultimatum to Belgium demanding a free passage for her troops, through to France. This threat resolved the hesitations of the British Government, which now despatched an ultimatum that Germany should honour her pledges to respect Belgian neutrality. No satisfactory answer was possible—the inflexibility and intricacy of the military machine forbade it. Bethmann-Hollweg complained that Britain was going to war "just for a scrap of paper."

At eleven o'clock on the night of August 4th, the ultimatum expired—and Britain also was in the war. The German troops had already crossed the Belgian frontier. Only one of the Great Powers of Europe had managed for the moment, to keep out of it—Italy: by her decision to cut loose from her engagements to Germany and Austria.

2. THE POWDER

The outbreak of war in 1914 set in motion forces more gigantic than any war had seen. Two million Germans were on the march, the greater part against France, and there were another three million trained men to back them up. France had nearly four million trained men at call, although she relied only on a million of the active troops in the first clash. Russia had more millions to draw upon than any, but her mobilization process was slower, a large part of her forces were in Asia, and her eventual strength was hampered by lack of munitions.

The growth of these immense forces had been due primarily to a military gospel of mass. Proclaimed by Clausewitz, the Prussian military philosopher, who drew his inspiration from Napoleon's example, the spread of this gospel had been stimulated by the victories of the Prussian conscript armies in 1866 against Austria and 1870 against France. Also it had been assisted by the development of railways, which enabled far larger numbers of men to be assembled and supplied. Thus the armies of 1914-1918 came to be counted in their millions compared with the hundreds of thousands of half a century earlier.

The military minds of Europe had a too absorbing faith in one of Napoleon's sayings, so often contradictory, that victory lay with the "big battalions." It had led to a relative neglect of scientific progress and technical invention: to an underrating of the value of weapon-power compared with mere man-power. On the eve of the twentieth century, one of the most eminent military teachers in Europe, Colonel Foch, had declared, "that any improvement in firearms is bound to strengthen the offensive." The coming war was to prove the opposite.

Foch's deduction, even when made, was contrary to the evidence of the American Civil War, the first modern war—which no soldiers in Europe save the British deemed to be worth study. It was contrary, also, to facts which might have been discovered by dispassionate analysis of the briefer wars of 1864, 1866 and 1870. And it was subsequently contradicted by the experience of the South African and Russo-Japanese Wars. Here the ominous shadow of the machine-gun —"concentrated essence of infantry"—began to creep across the battlefield, bringing movement to a standstill. Some of the more acute foreign observers who were actually present at these wars perceived this paralysing trend, but their voices had slight echo in the War Ministries of Europe, where the military chiefs existed in monastic seclusion chanting the creed of Clausewitz before the altar of Napoleon.

One of these onlookers, the youthful Captain Hoffmann, succeeded in making sufficient impression on the German authorities to induce them to pay some attention to the machine-gun, and also to provide themselves with mobile heavy artillery as an aid to overcoming modern defence.

The average proportion of machine-guns in the chief European armies of 1914 was only two to a thousand men. In several armies it was less. Yet experience was soon to show that two machine-guns in defence were often capable of paralysing the attacking power of a thousand men, driving them to take refuge in trenches. And as machine-guns became more plentiful, together with barbed wire and entrenchments, the paralysis would become more severe.

It was intensified by another flaw which the gospel of mass revealed under test. The military chiefs, in their anxiety to swell their ranks, had forgotten the warning of the most sagacious of their eighteenth-century predecessors, Marshal Saxe, that—"Multitudes serve only to perplex and embarrass." Even with the aid of the railway, it was difficult to handle armies of millions, to keep them supplied, and to prevent them clogging the arteries of movement. Their very mass stultified the dreams of Napoleonic manœuvres in which their creators had indulged. Napoleon's dazzling campaigns in Italy were aptly christened by Hilaire Belloc—"lightning in the hills." There was to be a lot of thunder, but little lightning, in the efforts of his would-be imitators in 1914-1918.

Their inability to control the forces they had called forth was ominously revealed before the war itself actually opened. Indeed, it precipitated the war: not merely by the fears which such swollen forces generated among the peoples.

The mobilization summons that drew the massed manhood of a nation from their civil avocations, to don uniform and gather at their war stations, produced a state of nervous excitement which drowned the voice of reason and wrecked the delicate process of negotiation.

In comparison, a professional force has the quality of constant yet unprovocative readiness, and is thus no more menace at a crisis than at a time of quietude. The unnoticed sailing of the Grand Fleet for its war station at Scapa offers a significant contrast to the furore caused by the mobilization of the great Continental armies.

Once the wheels of mobilization began to move, no brake could effectively retard them. Nor was the machine even steerable. Its rigid look was revealed when the Kaiser, clutching at a report that the French might agree to forsake their Russian allies, said to Moltke, the Chief of the German General Staff: "Now we can march, with all our forces, towards the East alone." Moltke replied "that this was impossible. The advance of armies formed of millions of men . . . was the result of years of painstaking work. Once planned, it could not possibly be changed." The Kaiser bitterly retorted: "Your uncle (the victor of 1870) would have given me a different reply."

Moltke gained his way, and the German armies continued their concentration against France. As a small concession, twenty-four hours delay in the actual crossing of the frontier was imposed, and even this led the German military chief to record: "It was a great shock to me, as though something had struck at my heart." His pathetic exclamation vividly illustrates the rigid limitations of the military machine as well as of the military mind.

In a survey of the war, the German war-plan must take priority. Not only was it the mainspring which set in motion the hands of the war clock in 1914, but, in a sense, it governed the course of the war thereafter. For, although it miscarried, it left the German army so deeply embedded in the land of France that the strategy of the Allies was henceforth loaded with, and narrowed by, the instinctive urge to evict it—a serious handicap to any less direct form of action which sober reasoning might suggest.

Geography gave Germany and her ally the advantage of a central position. This fact, together with Russia's proverbial slowness, guided Germany's opening moves. Her long-framed plan was to strike heavily and rapidly against France, while holding at bay Russia's advanced forces; and then, when France was crushed, to deal with the Russians. The obvious hindrance to such an aim was the obstacle offered by the strong fortress system along the French frontier. To force it spelt a loss of time, and time was the one thing that the Germans felt they could not afford to lose. So they had decided to go round the obstacle—by a wide manœuvre through Belgium. This plan was definitely adopted in 1905 by Count Schlieffen, then Chief of the German General Staff. He considered that the military advantages outweighed the moral stigma of violating Belgian neutrality, and also the practical dangers of British hostility.

Schlieffen's plan concentrated the mass of the German forces on the right (the western) wing for a gigantic wheel through Belgium and northern France, while the minimum force was allotted to the left wing facing the French eastern frontier. Dying before the war, Schlieffen's last words are said to have been: "it must come to a fight. Only make the right wing strong." If the French forces took the offensive against the German left wing, its very weakness would be an asset. Like a revolving door, the more heavily the Frenchman pressed on one side, the more forcefully would the other side swing round behind him. Here lay the subtlety of the plan, not in the mere geographical detour. Even Schlieffen seems to have been unconscious of its full subtlety, while Moltke endangered its effect by strengthening the left wing armies to an extent which encouraged their commanders to turn about and take the offensive too early.

The French war-plan fitted into the German plan ideally—from a German point of view. It was due to a new school of theorists, pupils of Foch, who were intoxicated with the French tradition of the offensive and had deluded themselves into the semi-mystical belief that all virtue lay in the offensive, that they had only to attack with enough ardour to be sure of conquering. In 1912 they unseated the Chief of the General Staff, General Michel, who expected the Germans to come through Belgium and was anxious to meet the menace by defensive preparations. In his place was appointed a stolid general, Joffre, who promised to be a stout lever for their designs. Under the cloak of his authority, they moulded the French doctrine and plan towards a headlong offensive. Believing that reservists were not capable of such an effort, they relied only on the active troops. And, partly to strengthen their case, they counted only the German active troops— whereas the Germans had blended both kinds in their striking force. In consequence a million Frenchmen advanced to meet a million and a half Germans—and advanced in the wrong place.

1914

1. THE INVASION OF FRANCE

Before the armies of the German right wing could make their scythe-like sweep through France they needed elbow-room to swing the scythe. For this, as they had abandoned the idea of crossing the "Maastricht appendix" of Holland, they had first to squeeze through the narrow passage between the Ardennes and the Dutch frontier. The forts of Liége commanded this passage; and to clear it, if the Belgians offered resistance, the German plan had provided an advance detachment, drawn from the normal frontier force. This hurried forward on August 5th and part of it penetrated between the forts during the night, then pushing on to seize the city. The success of the coup owed much to the initiative of a staff officer, soon to become famous as General Ludendorff, who had come to watch but took the lead when he found that the advance was faltering. The forts, however, held out until the Germans brought up their heavy howitzers, and ten days elapsed before the passage was effectively cleared.

The Belgian field army had been deployed across the path beyond, but now withdrew to the flank, at Antwerp, after vainly appealing to its allies for support. With the check thus removed, the Germans poured rapidly into the Belgian plain, deployed, swept forward, and reached the French frontier up to

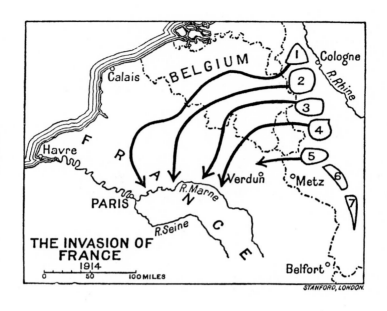

Calais

BELGIUM

Cologne

R. Rhine

1

2

3

4

5

Metz

6

7

F

R

A

N

C

E

Havre

Verdun

R. Marne

PARIS

R. Seine

Belfort

THE INVASION OF
FRANCE
1914

0   50   100 MILES

STANFORD, LONDON.

time-table. But they might have been four or five days ahead of it, if they had been given a free pass at Liége. Greater effects still were to come from the Belgians' demolition of the communications that the advancing masses needed for their supply.

France would have fared badly without this indirect aid, for folly had jeopardized her security. Not even the fall of Liége, the gateway into western Belgium, could awaken the intoxicated French Command to reality. If they had sent a few army corps to reinforce the defence that their small ally was offering, there is little doubt that the Germans might have been held up on the threshold, along the line Namur-Antwerp. But the French were intent only on pressing their own dream offensive. Thus while the Germans were sweeping through Belgium, the French, on August 14th, hurled their two right wing armies across the Lorraine frontier of Germany—into a trap. From this they recoiled in disorder, shaken by the discovery that the "will to conquer" did not suffice to make them invulnerable against modern weapons. The defeat was precipitated because the faith of their leaders in the offensive had made them careless of normal precautions.

Fortunately for them, the leaders on the German left wing there were only a degree less ardent for the offensive, and had wrung from a weak Supreme Command permission to take the counter-offensive at the first opportunity instead of drawing the French on further, as intended. As a consequence, the French suffered their reverse before they had advanced too

far, and were able to regain their fortified frontier
where they rallied in shelter. Also, this barrier augmented the resisting power of the forces which held
it, so that the French Commander-in-Chief, Joffre, was
able to send part of them to reinforce the western end
of his line. This transfer of forces, which had mo-
mentous effects in changing the balance of the war,
was called for by the crisis—indeed, the series of crises
—which arose on the other flank.

When the French had belatedly awoken to the fact
that the Germans were coming through Belgium—
although even then they did not realize the full width
of the sweep—they jumped to the conclusion that the
German centre must be thin. This delusion was fos-
tered by their own underestimate of the forces that
the enemy was employing. And it lured them to
hasten their second stroke, also by two armies, in the
effort to exploit the opening.

On August 21st, a week after Joffre's right hand
blow in Lorraine and the day after its defeat, he
struck a left hand blow at the supposedly weak German centre in Belgian Luxembourg, between the
Moselle and the Meuse. For his information he relied
mainly on his cavalry, of which he had one hundred
thousand, but "this enormous mass of cavalry discovered nothing of the enemy's advance . . . and the
French armies were everywhere surprised." Blunder-
ing forward into the wooded Ardennes, they ran slant-
wise into the advancing Germans and suffered a fresh
defeat. Fortunately for them, the Germans, also rely-

ing on cavalry who proved equally useless, failed to realize or exploit the opportunity.

But in western Belgium, beyond the Meuse, three German armies (thirty-four divisions) were rapidly closing upon the French Fifth Army (ten divisions) on the extreme left, and the little British Expeditionary Force of four divisions alongside it. These forces were intended by Joffre to envelop the German right wing: instead, they were themselves outflanked as well as outnumbered. Their plight would have been even more perilous but for Lanrezac, the commander of the Fifth Army. He had suspected the wideness of the German sweep, and although his arguments failed to convince Joffre, his insistence had gained permission for his army to move further to the west before joining in the offensive. It was due to this side-step, and to the arrival of the British on his exposed western flank at Mons, that the enemy's encircling move miscarried. Nevertheless, it would seem that if the British had not moved so far inland, to link up with the French, they might have thrown the German machine out of gear more definitely, and at less risk to themselves. For until they were actually met, Kluck, the commander of the German First Army on the right, was "so obsessed" with the fear that the British might appear from the coast on his outer flank that his advance was marked by hesitation, even halting at rumours. The course of his advance accorded with the common experience of war that moves become surer, and movements accelerated, in proportion to knowledge of the opponent's situation.

On August 23rd, Lanrezac, who had already been deprived of the crossings of the Sambre in his front by the German Second Army, heard that the Third Army was behind his right flank: in consequence he ordered his army to retire, beginning that night. When the news reached the British Commander-in-Chief, Sir John French, whose troops had been resisting superior odds all day, he issued similar orders. Early next morning both armies were marching southward.

2. THE RETREAT FROM THE FRONTIERS

All the French armies were now in retreat. The retreat of the four main armies had been under the compulsion of defeat, and only the two on the right had a fortified line to help them in making a stand and holding the frontier. The two that were recoiling from the Ardennes were carried back far into France by the inflowing tide; of these, the Third Army clung by its right arm to the fortress of Verdun, which now began to project like a breakwater into the grey waves, but the Fourth began to split up under the double strain of clinging to its neighbour and resisting the tide.

On the extreme left, the Fifth Army and the British had fallen back just in time to avert disaster. Even so, they were not out of danger—which was gravest on the exposed left wing of the British. Here Smith-Dorrien, whose corps had been closely pressed, decided that it was impossible to continue the retreat as ordered. So at Le Cateau on August 26th, the anniversary of Crécy, his corps stood at bay, facing heavy odds. Its peril was the greater because its right flank was also exposed, owing to the fact that Haig's corps had not only continued its retreat but taken a divergent direction, due southward instead of south-westward—this being inspired by the exaggerated impression made on Haig by a chance skirmish at dusk near his headquarters. He jumped to the conclusion, a pure delusion, that his situation was "very critical," and his repeated appeals for help led Sir John French to suggest that his corps should take refuge with the French. On top of this French heard of Smith-Dorrien's decision to make a stand, and he felt that disaster was inevitable. The next day French seems to have "given up the II Corps as lost."

Luckily for Smith-Dorrien his German opponent was also labouring under a confused idea of the situation, and exerted only a small part of his strength, so that Smith-Dorrien's battered corps was able to slip away in the evening. And next day the Germans, continuing under a false impression, continued their pursuit in the wrong direction, believing that the British were retiring to the coast. If they thereby missed their quarry, their wide south-westerly sweep had an important strategic effect.

With the news that all his armies were in retreat, Joffre had at last awakened to the reality of the situation. Whatever his defects of vision he was not lacking in resolution. Reshuffling his hand, he drew troops from his right wing, which was covered by the Lorraine fortress barrier, in order to create on his left a new striking force that he could use against the enemy's marching flank. Sent by rail, these troops began to assemble in the Somme area on the 28th. But the Germans were once again moving wider than he had expected—and this second plan collapsed like a pack of cards. Finding themselves caught within the sweep of the enemy's scythe, the newly formed Sixth Army had to fall back and seek shelter within the fortified zone of Paris.

But the German plan now began to crack—under the excitable pressure of unsteady hands. The successes in the first clash on the frontier had been swelled in the reports of the army commanders, each zealous to glorify his own achievement, and the compound effect had unbalanced Moltke, who was in supreme command. He was but the shadow of his famous uncle except in physical bulk, and the state of his health affected the state of his mind. Fresh from undergoing a cure, he had almost collapsed under the weight of responsibility before the invasion had even begun. Revived by the stimulus of intoxicating reports he was carried away into rosy illusions before finally going to pieces when the prospect faded.

The impression that "a decisive victory" had already been won coincided with the news of an emergency on the Russian front, and Moltke decided on the 25th that he could now afford to settle the issue there and detailed six army corps for that purpose. Two had actually gone before he heard that the Russians had been decisively beaten at Tannenberg: these two had been occupied in reducing the Belgian fortress of Namur, whose last forts fell on the 25th. Moltke weakened his right wing still more by detailing a large fraction to watch over the Belgians and guard against a possible menace to his communications. By retiring to a flank, instead of retreating in front of the Germans, the Belgian army had multiplied its potential effect; and this was multiplied again by the fear that the British would reinforce it by sea.

The blame for the ultimate German failure has been generally thrown, for a generation, on Moltke's neglect to obey his predecessor's admonition: "Keep the right wing strong." The impression was certainly strengthened by the fact that when the decisive test came, on the Marne, there were only thirteen divisions on that flank against double the number—simple arithmetic largely influences military judgment. But there were deeper causes.

The German masses imposed a heavy strain on their own means of supply. These in turn were strained to breaking-point by the Belgians' destruction of the bridges over the Meuse—no trains could run past Liége until August 24th and then only by an awkward deviation: and even when the German marching columns had reached the Marne, the supplies of all three armies on the right had to pass through this one half-strangled artery. That blockage was also the decisive factor in making it impossible for the Germans to reinforce their right wing with troops from their left, according to the original plan—although it would have been useless to multiply numbers unless they could have been fed. Mass gave momentum to a vicious circle. It becomes clear—by *strategic* arithmetic—that in this supreme crisis of the war a handful of Belgian engineers on the Meuse counted for more than several army corps on the Marne.

The German generals, especially Kluck, increased the weakness of their own situation by pushing their men forward so fast that they even ran away from such supplies as they had. The troops had to forage for what they could find in a countryside exhausted of provisions. For several days they obtained little more to eat than an occasional cup of soup and piece of bread, eked out by raw turnips and unripe fruit. Hunger combined with the fatigue of forced marches in August heat to reduce them to a dead-beat condition. Small forces of picked men can march stripped and remain efficient—not masses. To make matters worse, Moltke lost touch with his army commanders—owing to lack of foresight in preparing means of communication, and to the indiscriminate way his cavalry had destroyed the telegraph system in France. Thus, in sum, so much grit had worked into the German machine that a slight jar would suffice to cause its breakdown. This was delivered in the so-called "battle" of the Marne.

The opportunity was offered by the German right wing wheeling inwards before Paris was reached, thereby exposing its flank to a counter-stroke. The opportunity was grasped, not by Joffre, but by Galliéni, the governor of Paris. The French main armies

were continuing their retreat southward when Galliéni moved the Paris garrison forward against the
enemy's flank and induced Joffre, after a day-long
argument, to support him by ordering a general turn-
about.

3. THE BATTLE OF THE MARNE

On August 30th Joffre was driven to abandon the
project of building up a new mass to envelop the
Germans' flank, since on that day he had been forced
to part with its nucleus, the Sixth Army—as a reinforcement to the Paris garrison. Instead, he pinned
his faith to a new design of breaking the German
centre. But this idea in turn began to crumble, as the
enemy pressure developed and his retreating forces
threatened to get out of control. On September 1st
he ordered the retreat to be continued to a line south
of the Seine, saying that it was impossible to make a
stand on the Marne. Although a captured map was
brought to him that evening, which as he himself later
admitted, "made it perfectly clear" that Kluck was
changing direction, it did not change his own intention to continue retreating. The next day, in a note
to his army commanders, he indicated a line still further south—a line, moreover, where they would "for-
tify themselves" and await "drafts from the depots."
In Joffre's own words: "The state of our men, as reported by the army commanders, gave additional reason for inclining to this solution." Joffre's chief ad-

visers were in agreement on this. The most influential,
General Berthelot, held that "the troops were so worn
out by the long retreat which had never ceased since
the Sambre, that they were incapable of making any
effort."

Galliéni was left to discover for himself—late on the
3rd—that the Germans were changing direction and
moving across his front. But he was quick to see the
chance that offered, and early next morning ordered
his forces to get ready for a stroke against them. In-
forming Joffre by telephone of what he had done, he
urged him to sanction a counter-offensive. Some of the
younger men on Joffre's staff backed up the idea, but
Berthelot was firm for continued retreat. Joffre hesitated to go against his judgment, although after Galliéni's intervention he had been moved so far as to
telegraph an enquiry to Franchet d'Esperey—whom
he had put in Lanrezac's place as Commander of the
Fifth Army—whether "your army is in a state to attack with any chance of success?" Just before it
reached Franchet d'Esperey, the latter had issued orders for his army to retreat to the Seine "as quickly
as possible."

Then in the afternoon ominous news from the
flank of the Fifth Army reinforced Berthelot's arguments, and Joffre was inclined to feel that the counter-
offensive must be "delayed for five or six days" at
least. "I decided that I would once more move my
headquarters to the rear"—actually the order was
given to move them over eighty miles back. This is a
fact which makes it hard to believe subsequent claims

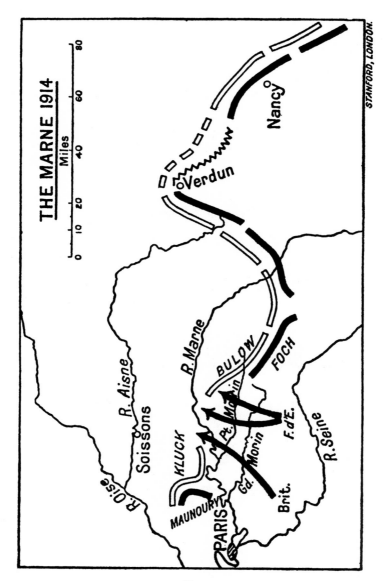

THE MARNE 1914

Miles

STANFORD, LONDON.

41

that Joffre had still any thought of taking the counter-offensive.

At dinner he heard that important papers had arrived from the Fifth Army, and as soon as it was finished he went to headquarters to see them. He found that they contained Franchet d'Esperey's long-awaited reply. The formal note briefly said: "The battle cannot begin before the day after to-morrow, September 6th," adding that the Fifth Army would continue its withdrawal on the morrow to a line whence it might take the offensive. But it was accompanied by a qualifying note in Franchet d'Esperey's own hand, which warned Joffre: "My army can fight on the 6th but its situation is far from brilliant. No reliance can be placed on the reserve divisions." In later years Joffre declared that this note filled him with joy—but it is not easy to understand how so dubious a note had so comforting an effect. It is more easy to appreciate that he wanted to forget the influence of what took place just after.

For while he was still studying Franchet d'Esperey's messages he heard that Galliéni was on the telephone and insisted on speaking to him personally. Joffre had such a dislike of the telephone that, according to his aide-de-camp, this was about the only occasion he ever consented to speak on it. But Galliéni was his old chief—in Madagascar, was the most illustrious soldier of France, and had proposed Joffre for the commander-in-chief when forgoing it himself from a scruple of honour. What passed between them will never be known with certainty. Galliéni, according to his staff and secretaries, vehemently urged Joffre to take the counter-offensive and by the force of his arguments gained Joffre's assent. Joffre, according to his own account, told Galliéni that he had already made up his mind to take the counter-offensive, and that his plan was now in accord with Galliéni's proposals of the morning. Joffre's aide-de-camp, however, has disclosed that there was an argument, and that Galliéni evidently used an emphatic tone. He admits, too, that it was only then that Joffre took the definite decision. Apart from this evidence, the run of the facts tends to confirm the view that Joffre was decisively influenced by "his master's voice."

There was reason afterwards for denying the suggestion, since Joffre needed the laurels of the Marne to cover the ashes of his opening plans, while Galliéni had been nominated by the Government as his prospective successor. And the longer that laurels are kept the harder it is to part with them. In such circumstances human memory has convenient blanks. Indeed, when the controversy waxed fierce in later years, after Galliéni's death, Joffre went so far as to declare at one time that he had "no recollection" of even having any conversation on the telephone!

Although Galliéni's orders to the Sixth Army were issued at 8-30 p.m., Joffre's were not sent out until several hours later—another significant fact. They did not reach the armies until the early hours of the 5th: both Franchet d'Esperey and the British felt that it was too late to make a change, so their armies continued the retreat for another day—while the Sixth Army was moving against the enemy's flanks.

Galliéni's stroke temporarily unhinged the German right wing; Kluck was taken by surprise, having sent out no air reconnaissance to watch his exposed flank. And now, when taken off his guard, the "disappearance" of the British encouraged him in a freshly dangerous delusion. For having pulled back half his army to meet the flank threat, he was now emboldened to draw off the remainder in the hope of retrieving his initial set-back by winning a local victory. Thereby he left a gap of thirty miles, covered only by a screen of cavalry, between himself and his neighbour, Bülow.

The British columns had turned about on the 6th and were marching north, but not fast enough to warn Kluck until, on the morning of the 9th, they were suddenly reported to be moving into the gap. The news of their unexpected reappearance at this crucial point came at a moment when the German leaders were nerve-racked by rumours that many thousands of British and Russians were disembarking on the Belgian coast in their rear—in reality, a mere three thousand marines sent by Mr. Winston Churchill, the First Lord of the Admirality, as a bluff. The fresh moral shock cracked the nerve of the German command. With its approval, the armies of Bülow and Kluck fell back in hasty retreat.

At the other end of the Western Front, an attempt to force the French fortified frontier had ended the previous day in costly failure. In the centre the Crown

Prince's attempt to break past the Verdun pivot had collapsed under the torrential fire of the French artillery, who found in defence against massed attacks a better opportunity than in their own offensive. The one point of serious danger to the French armies was on Franchet d'Esperey's right, where Foch, newly given command of an army, disobeyed instructions through excess of offensive zeal. Instead of covering his neighbour's flank as ordered, he concentrated his forces for an attacking stroke on his left, while weakening his own exposed right. The Germans pushed in here and Foch's flank collapsed. He hurriedly called for help, with the result that he subtracted from the strength of the main offensive which he had been intended to protect. With the reinforcements that were sent him he launched a counter-stroke, which became legendary as the decisive turn of the Battle of the Marne. But, in fact, the Germans had vanished before it developed—having been recalled by Bülow's order for a general retirement.

With his right wing disjointed, his left wing held up, and his forces beyond his control, Moltke was merely a distant spectator of the retreat which now began. The tide of invasion had turned, rolling back from Paris and the Marne.

For a few days the Allies had the chance of converting the retreat into a serious defeat, but they followed it up so cautiously that the Germans were able to re-knit their right wing on the Aisne.

4. THE ADVANCE TO THE AISNE

The capacity of the Allies did not equal their confidence. On September 12th Berthelot and Henry Wilson, the guiding brains of two headquarters, discussed the probable date of crossing the German frontier. The British general estimated it at four weeks hence: the Frenchman put it a week earlier.

The Allied leaders had not been so quick in pursuit as in prophecy. Sir John French did not enlighten his troops as to the greatness of their opportunity nor the importance of speed, even when Joffre belatedly emphasized it. The British advance averaged barely nine miles a day. On the 8th four British infantry and two cavalry divisions were held up on the Petit Morin for the greater part of the day by a couple of German battalions and a handful of dismounted cavalry, with ten machine-guns. On the 9th, after crossing the Marne, Haig halted his corps for several hours until his aircraft reported "all clear." Then, just as he was cautiously resuming the advance, French intervened to stop it for the rest of the day. The cavalry were kept behind the infantry, and went into billets in the afternoon—when a mass of German transport lay just ahead, inviting capture.

On the following days the opportunity grew rather than diminished, because the gap between the two German armies increased. The two Allied armies had now penetrated right between them. The Allied leaders were aware of the gap, and also that with the fall of Maubeuge fresh German troops might shortly arrive to fill it. There was no time to lose. Joffre's orders now sounded a note of urgency, and French on the 12th gave rein to his cavalry. But after advancing a mere seven miles, these stopped and went into billets —although the Aisne lay only seven miles beyond. Haig, too, put the brake on: although he had specific orders to seize the crossings, he had a fresh fit of caution during the day and ordered his divisions not to proceed as far as the river.

Franchet d'Esperey's advance had been hardly less cautious. His right wing, diverted to Foch's assistance, slowly followed but did not seriously press Bülow's army as it wheeled back. His centre and left wing failed to push along the wide path that was thrown open to them. Then, on reaching the Aisne, Conneau's cavalry corps found itself opposite a yawning gap in the German front. Riding through this, it was forty miles in rear of the general line of the German armies, whose communications thus lay exposed to dislocation. Instead of seizing the opportunity the French cavalry only saw their own possible danger, and ingloriously retired.

The British also had an opportunity, if not so great, left to them when they reached the Aisne on the 13th. But, in the words of the Official History, this was forfeited owing to "a failure of the Higher Command to appreciate the situation."

That day Haig's corps "made a rather cautious and leisurely advance" and "in the G.H.Q. orders there was no hint whatever of the value of time." By next day German reserves had arrived from Maubeuge to fill the gap, and such hope as was left depended on a properly organized attack. Instead "there was no plan, no objective, no arrangements for co-operation, and the divisions blundered into battle."

Thus the Germans were able to reknit their front. And now the machine-gun began to reveal its full power, cementing the line into an impenetrable barrier. Slow to realize his opportunity Joffre was slow to realize that it had passed. On the very day that his advance was blocked he telegraphed to the Government: "Our victory is pronouncing itself more and more complete and brilliant. . . . Our advanced guards are treading on the heels of the enemy without giving him a moment to pull himself together." Because of his tardy awakening to reality, he wasted several days before he began to grope for an open flank. His manœuvre, which was christened with unconscious irony "the race to the sea," was carried out by successive sidesteps north-westward, each so narrow and so obvious that the Germans had no difficulty in forestalling them—until by October the movement came to rest on the sea, and the entrenched front stretched from the Swiss frontier to the English Channel.

5. THE STRUGGLE AT YPRES

Although the presence of the Belgian Army at Antwerp was a standing menace to the German communications, Joffre did not think of developing it and stoutly resisted the idea of sending French reinforcements thither. But the Germans were acutely sensitive to the danger, and while Joffre was ponderously side-stepping, they concentrated forces to extract this thorn from their side. On September 28th their guns began the bombardment of Antwerp. They had an echo in England, if not in France. Mr. Winston Churchill, the First Lord of the Admiralty, had already been urging the importance of reinforcing the Belgians, but although there were eleven territorial divisions available, Lord Kitchener, who had become War Minister, did not regard them as yet fit for an active role. On Churchill's initiative a scratch force of marines and naval volunteers, many of them still less trained, was rushed across the Channel and sent up to Antwerp, while Kitchener was arranging to send a regular infantry and cavalry division. The belated reinforcement was too meagre to prevent the fall of Antwerp but it helped the Belgian army to slip safely away, down the coast. Moreover, it gained time that proved the salvation of the Channel ports of France.

For Falkenhayn, who had replaced Moltke, was planning a great sweep down the coast while Joffre was pursuing his narrow series of outflanking movements. Even before the Battle of the Marne Falkenhayn had urged on Moltke "the necessity of occupying the north coast," but Moltke had firmly clung to the Clausewitzian faith that nothing else counted beside winning the "decisive battle." So the ports that were vital for Britain's communication with France were left untouched during the weeks that the Germans could have had them for the picking. Falkenhayn's horizon was not so narrowly bounded, and now that he was in charge he was eager to retrieve the lost opportunity, as soon as he had cleared his communications. But Antwerp did not fall until October 10th and nearly a week more elapsed before the German forces thus released, reinforced by four newly raised army corps, began their drive from the coast.

Meantime Joffre had unwittingly tried to allow them a clear path. Obsessed with his dream of outflanking the main German armies, he had sought to induce the Belgians to leave the coast and march inland to join his imagined decisive wing. But King Albert did not yield to his arguments, even when it was reinforced by the personal persuasion of Foch, who had been sent to Flanders, as Joffre's deputy, to co-ordinate the manœuvre. Foch eloquently declared to the King: "At the moment when we are setting out on the conquest of Belgium, people will not understand why the Belgian army is not figuring alongside us. For myself I can assure your Majesty that our cause is just and holy, and that Providence will give us the victory."

It was fortunate that the Belgian army had stayed to guard the path down the coast. For, on the heels of this assurance its line on the Yser was struck by a flood of Germans pouring down from Antwerp. After ten days of crisis the Belgians stemmed it on the 28th by opening the locks and letting in a flood from the sea.

This forced the Germans to throw all their weight inland, in the Ypres sector. Here the Allied defence had been formed fortuitously by the arrival of the

main British army which had been transferred from
the Aisne to serve together with a French army as the
left tip of Joffre's latest outflanking manœuvre. On
reaching Ypres Haig's corps duly began its advance
only to be thrown instantly on the defensive by the
German offensive, simultaneously unloosed. For several days Foch and French, sublimely disregarding
reality, went on issuing orders to "continue the advance"—while their troops were barely holding the
ground. When the two chiefs came to understand that
they were suffering attack, not making it, they found
fresh cause for optimism in the temporary slackening
of the onslaught. French wired to Kitchener: "The
enemy are vigorously playing their last card." On the
24th, ordering his own offensive to be resumed, he
wired again that the battle was "practically won."
When this failed, he wired that the Germans "were
quite incapable of making any strong and sustained
attack."

Instead, from the 29th onwards a series of heavy
blows crashed on the thin British line. The first day it
only made a crack at one point. On the second it broke
into the southern flank of the British, making a jagged
hole that was precariously filled by such scanty reserves as the British and French could find. On the
third day Haig's centre was broken. Haig was driven
to issue orders for his troops to fall back, while French,
who had come to see him at the blackest moment, hurried back to his car and drove despairingly to beg help
of the French, having none to offer himself. Foch su-
perbly replied, if his memory were accurate: "Mar-

shal, your lines are pierced. You have no troops available. Then you must advance." French found more comfort in a promise that fresh French reserves would launch a counter-attack to relieve the pressure.

Happily, the situation had already been saved—for, having broken through, the Germans did not know how to exploit their success and when still in confusion were tumbled back by a local British counter-attack. The French counter-attack next day did not fulfil Foch's promise. On the southern flank the Messines ridge was lost. French reserves now came up in growing numbers, and they took over the southern flank before the German offensive swelled afresh, to reach its climax on November 11th—a prophetic date. Two fresh breaches were made that day but the Germans failed to profit by their opportunity.

The storm now at last subsided. Defence had triumphed over attack—the kind of attack on which, before the war, all the General Staffs had counted confidently for success. It was baffled by the bullet, not by any new agent, nor even by the more modern forms of bullet-projection. To the dazed German troops it seemed that from "every bush, hedge and fragment of wall" there was "a machine-gun rattling out bullets." But in fact the British, starting the war with few, had been reduced to still fewer by the time they arrived in Flanders. To make up for the scarcity they depended on their rifle-shooting with which, after the lesson given them by the Boers, they had been trained to produce "fifteen rounds rapid" in the minute.

But the poverty of their resources and the delusions

of the Allied chiefs had increased the strain on the desperately thin line—"of tired, haggard and unshaven men, unwashed, plastered with mud, many in little more than rags"—which stood between the Germans and their goal. After resisting a rain of attacks for a month there was little left of the original British Expeditionary Force. The defence of Ypres was the monument to the Regular Army—over its grave. Of its fighting men too few survived to season their successors.

Its higher leaders, however, would remain to take over charge of greater hosts than they had ever imagined. For back at home, a million volunteers had already come forward at Kitchener's call, and the New Armies of Britain were springing up. How little the prospect impressed some of their future users is shown by Henry Wilson's comment in mid-September: "Kitchener's ridiculous and preposterous army of twenty-five corps is the laughing-stock of every soldier in Europe . . . under no circumstances could these mobs take the field for two years. Then what is the use of them?" The New Armies were allowed time to grow because of the state of deadlock—also unforeseen—which now ruled on the Western Front. But they were ready for their baptism of fire within nine months of conception. It is true that they might have been better prepared to meet the conditions which then faced them—but that was not their fault.

6. THE RUSSIAN FRONT

On the Russian front meantime a series of rapid reversals of fortune had ended in a similar deadlock, if one that was less firmly established. Conrad von Hötzendorf, the Austrian chief, had desired to cut off the Russian forces in the protruding Polish "tongue"—by a combined offensive of the Germans from the north side and the Austrians from the south. But his allies, despite vague assurances, were disinclined to move until they had settled with France: and, on August 20th, he, rashly, took the offensive alone.

Lemberg. Advancing blindly—since his great mass of cavalry proved useless as eyes—he collided with one half of the main Russian forces, who were also advancing southward. The Russian commanders, however, were equally surprised, having a picture of the enemy's movement that was the exact opposite of the reality. Thereby they got in a knot, and Conrad had a chance to encircle them.

At this moment the other half of the Russian armies, advancing westward, crashed into his weak flank near Lemberg. Fortunately for him they halted, being still under the influence of their false opening picture. Recovering from his surprise, Conrad tried to turn the tables on his assailants by a series of strategic juggles, which imposed a greater strain on his own cumbersome forces than they could safely bear. They began to

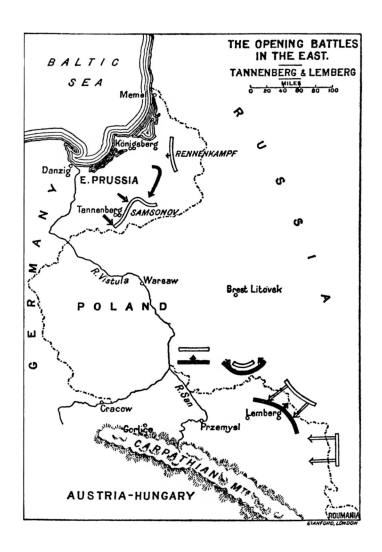

THE OPENING BATTLES
IN THE EAST.

TANNENBERG & LEMBERG

MILES
0 20 40 60 80 100

BALTIC
SEA

Memel

Königsberg

RENNENKAMPF

Danzig

E. PRUSSIA

Tannenberg

SAMSONOV

R. Vistula   Warsaw

Brest Litovsk

POLAND

GERMANY

RUSSIA

R. San

Cracow

Przemysl

Lemberg

Gorlice

CARPATHIAN MTS.

AUSTRIA-HUNGARY

ROUMANIA

STANFORD, LONDON

55

collapse and were in danger of being cut off when the folly of the Russians in sending out wireless orders unciphered revealed to Conrad that masses of Russians were closing on his line of retreat. This enabled him to fall back just in time. His forces, however, were so badly mauled that the retreat did not stop until they had fallen back one hundred and fifty miles. Within a month Conrad had lost the province of Galicia and 350,000 men—out of an original 900,000.

Tannenberg. On the Baltic side of Poland, the campaign had opened with a Russian advance which turned into a Russian disaster. To meet the urgent clamour of their French allies, the Russians had hastened their invasion of East Prussia. One army, under Rennenkampf, advanced westwards and was met near the frontier by the bulk of the German forces in the East. The forces were fairly equal and the issue hovered in the balance. Rennenkampf was about to retreat, because his flanks were being encircled, when he found that the Germans were already retreating.

For that same day another Russian army, under Samsonov, had crossed the southern border, thus threatening to move astride the German's rear. Prittwitz, the German commander, thereupon lost his head and telephoned to Moltke to announce that he was about to make a precipitate retreat. This led to his prompt supersession. Moltke looked round for a man of decision and picked Ludendorff, who had just won laurels at Liége. Since Ludendorff was comparatively junior in rank, he had to be provided with a titular chief, and for this function a retired general, Hindenburg, was chosen. The German army paid deference to seniority, but it had a way of getting over the handicap of senility by placing the real power in the hands of picked staff officers, without regard to their rank. After Ludendorff had conferred with Moltke and despatched his initial orders direct to the unfortunate Prittwitz's corps commanders, he caught the train for East Prussia, collecting Hindenburg on the way.

Meantime, one of Prittwitz's staff, Lieut-Colonel Hoffmann had initiated a series of moves by which Samsonov's army was to be caught and crushed at Tannenberg while Rennenkampf was slowly toiling forward with no enemy in front of him—for the German forces had been rushed back to strike at Samsonov's flank. Here, as so often later, the swift German moves were made sure by the Russian commanders' habit of sending out unciphered wireless orders that could be easily intercepted and read. To make matters worse there was no connection between the two Russian armies, no co-ordination of them by the Higher Command, and no good feeling between the two army commanders.

On the 26th Samsonov's right wing was thrown back in disorder, but was not followed up. Next day the left wing collapsed, yet also slipped away without disaster. But Samsonov pushed his centre deeper into the bag, and the German corps commander on the right, General von François, thereupon disregarded Ludendorff's restraining orders and stretched a cordon of posts across the rear. By the night of the 29th, the two and a half corps of the Russian centre were encircled in a ring of fire. A total of 90,000 prisoners were taken, and more would have been rounded up if Ludendorff had not interfered with the closing of the bag by a contradictory series of orders. But since opinion is formed on the surface, and history is slow to catch up legend, "Tannenberg" raised Hindenburg to the stature of a national hero, in whose shadow Ludendorff's military reputation swelled proportionately.

The Austrian disasters soon compelled the Germans to send forces southward, to check the ebb. In October Russia began to approach the full tide of her mobilized strength and the Commander-in-Chief, the Grand Duke Nicholas, formed a huge phalanx of seven armies for an advance through Poland towards Berlin. Allied hopes rose high as "the steam-roller" rolled ponderously forward. But Ludendorff (with Hoffmann in the background) dislocated it by deftly switching his forces round the northern flank and driving a wedge into the joint near Lodz. The move was helped by the network of railways inside the German frontier as well as by the Russians' continued habit of disclosing their moves on the ether.

The phalanx was paralysed, and pushed back towards Warsaw. Winter now came to freeze the flux, and the two sides settled down in trench-lines astride Poland.

7. THE WAR AT SEA

With the failure to achieve any decisive result, in the east or the west, the war changed its form—to that of a gigantic siege. New factors came to the fore.

Sea-power assumed its historic importance. Its effect was slower but surer than that with which Napoleonic dreamers had credited the armies. There was no lightning flash over the seas, striking down the opponent. Instead, sea-power acted like radium beneficial to those who were shielded, it destroyed the tissues of those who were exposed to it.

The German military leaders had shown little interest in the action of their own navy, and less concern with the possible influence of Britain's navy—so confident were they of quick and overwhelming victory on land. When Moltke had been asked whether he would like the German navy to prevent the passage of the British forces to the Continent, his attitude was reflected in his remark that it would be better to leave them to be swallowed up by his army "at the same time as the other enemies." The French were equally disparaging in their valuation of sea-power—when Colonel Repington had suggested in *The Times* that the aid of the British navy was "worth 500,000 bayonets to the French," Joffre and Foch "did not value it at one bayonet." The scent of battle was so strong in their nostrils that none of the Continental war-leaders could see far beyond their noses.

But it was not long before sea-power made itself felt. While the German High Seas Fleet stayed in its harbours, waiting for something to turn up that might offset the existing British superiority in battleship strength the British Grand Fleet in its northern bases exerted a largely invisible domination of the sea. Under cover of this Germany was stripped of her colonies and her commerce was swept from the sea-routes, which remained open for the passage of the merchant ships and transports of Britain and her allies.

The seizure of the German colonies assured that the Allies would have important assets for negotiations if the war went badly for them in the main theatres. But the process of capture suffered from the neglect of the Admiralty and the War Office to study this obvious problem before the war came. Then, expeditions were hurriedly improvised "without preparation or information," so that their own conduct suffered and the naval arrangements to protect trade were temporarily dislocated. A New Zealand expedition was early despatched to occupy Samoa, and an Australian expedition took New Guinea. Japan joined in the game, if not seriously in the war, by capturing Tsing-tao on the coast of China. In Africa, the opportunities were well spread. Togoland was taken in August. The Cameroons offered a harder obstacle and more than a year passed before this equatorial region was at last conquered by joint British and French forces. German Southwest Africa was conquered by an expedition organized by the South African Prime Minister, General Botha. Only a dozen years had passed since he had been in arms against Britain, but now he was steadfast in loyalty to the British Commonwealth and swiftly suppressed the rebellion of a disaffected section of the Boers. In November an expedition was sent from India against German East Africa, the largest and richest of Germany's colonies.   But the local commander, General von Lettow-Vorbeck, showed a resourcefulness that discounted the invaders' superior strength, and the expedition ended in a fiasco.

It was not until late in 1915 that the attempt was renewed on a greater scale—through the help of the South African Government. Another of Britain's old opponents, General Smuts, was placed in command of the forces assembled there. Conducting a drive from the north, he reached the railway, over three hundred miles distant, which ran between the coast and Lake Tanganyika, while a force under Van Deventer made a wide sweep further inland. These converging advances forced Lettow-Vorbeck to fall back into the southeast corner of the colony, but by utilizing the difficulties of the ground and the advantages of local knowledge, he escaped being cut off. After Smuts had left for England, where he joined the Imperial War Cabinet, Lettow-Vorbeck continued to hold out, waging a guerrilla campaign until the war ended. Starting with a bare five thousand men, only five per cent being Europeans, he had caused the employment of 130,000 enemy troops.

But command of the sea meant far more to Britain than the capture of the opponent's colonies. If the security of the sea-routes were endangered her power to sustain the struggle would be paralysed. Indeed, Britain's very existence depended on the flow of supplies along those arteries.

The short sight of German leadership had been shown, once again, in its failure to make adequate preparations to interfere with its opponent's normal use of the seas. The Germans' naval effort and expenditure had been largely concentrated on building battleships for a battle they would not risk. For direct attack on Britain's trade routes Germany had available at the outset only her few cruisers which were on foreign service. These gave much trouble in proportion to their numbers—enough to show what might have been done. Two light cruisers, the *Emden* in the East Indies and the *Karlsruhe* in the West Indies, sank or captured thirty-two merchant ships between them. At one time seventy-eight British cruisers were in chase of, or on patrol against the *Emden* before she was at last caught, on November 9th. A fresh danger had just developed when Admiral von Spee's armoured cruisers, after crossing the Pacific, scored an initial success by overwhelming Admiral Cradock's cruiser squadron near Coronel off the coast of Chile, but this was retrieved by the British Admiralty's surprise move in despatching two battle-cruisers from home in a dash to the South Atlantic. These met and sank Spee's ships off the Falkland Isles on December 8th.

By the end of the year the outer seas had been swept clear of German warships, and with the main German fleet bottled in the North Sea it seemed that the British had definitely achieved "command of the sea," and that their problem was now reduced to that of exerting economic pressure on Germany. But the very completeness of that success, coupled with the disappointment of hopes of early victory on land, now drove the Germans to study the problem of finding a means of counter-pressure. The oceans were barred to them— but ships only cross the ocean in order to reach a port. In the submarine the Germans now saw a means of short-circuiting Britain's sea-communications; a weapon with which, despite the enemy's surface superiority, they could operate against the approaches to her home ports.

They were confirmed in this trend of thought by the course of several early encounters on the surface. At the end of August Admiral Beatty's battle-cruiser squadron made a swoop into the Bight of Heligoland and sank several German light cruisers. In November and December the German battle-cruisers retorted with a couple of "tip-and-run" raids on the English coast, but when they tried a third in January 1915, they were caught by Beatty and severely punished, narrowly escaping annihilation. This experience damped the Germans' hope that, by waiting, they might eventually be able to wear down the enemy's superiority and take them at a disadvantage. Attrition strategy revealed its limitations and risks earlier on sea than on land.

So in February the Germans decided to open a submarine campaign against commerce. And because of the risks to the submarines if normal methods of "visit and search" were applied, they proclaimed the waters round the British Isles a war zone where all ships, enemy or neutral, would be sunk at sight. By that action they unwittingly helped to loosen the restrictions which Britain had imposed on her own use of economic pressure: she retorted to the German proclamation by claiming the right to intercept all ships suspected of carrying goods to Germany, and bring them into her own ports for search. This tightening of the ring caused serious difficulties with neutrals, the

United States especially, but Germany eased the friction by torpedoing the great liner *Lusitania* on May 7th, 1915. The drowning of 1100 civilians was a shock to humanity, and appealed more forcibly to American opinion than even the desolation of Belgium. It brought the American Government to recognize the possibility of participation in the war, although the immediate tension was relieved by Germany's promise to modify her submarine action.

From that time onward the tension between the United States and Britain caused by the blockade was to be relieved repeatedly by some fresh German act at sea. Meantime the economic pressure on Germany was gradually tightened. But it would not become a stronghold until America herself reinforced it.

Before the war, the prevailing idea of a short war had led governments and generals to discount economic forces. Few men believed that a modern nation could long endure the strain of a large-scale conflict. The supply of food and of funds, the supply and manufacture of munitions, were problems that had only been studied on brief estimates. But with the failure to reach a result in 1914, the nations bestirred themselves to develop their resources, and factories for munitions sprouted like mushrooms. Also the nations revealed a financial adaptability that dumbfounded prewar economists.

1915

1. PRELUDE TO 1915

With the repulse of the German attempt to break through at Ypres the trench barrier was consolidated from the Swiss frontier to the English Channel. Modern defence had triumphed over direct attack, and stalemate ensued. Wisdom might have counselled Germany, her bid for quick victory having failed, to seek peace on reasonably favourable terms, helped by the bargaining assets she possessed in her occupation of others' territory.

But her military leaders, despite their palpable blunders, were still in the ascendency: and their minds were drugged by Clausewitz's notion of "absolute war"—the fight to a finish theory which, beginning with the argument that "war is only a continuation of state policy by other means," ended by making policy the slave of strategy. These soldiers were all too deeply indoctrinated with this maxim: "To introduce into the philosophy of war a principle of moderation would be an absurdity. War is an act of violence pushed to its utmost bounds." Such a principle of force without limit and without calculation of cost was the negation of statesmanship. The Germans would drive on, where they could. They often chose the point with shrewd judgment—but without any clear idea where it might lead them.

But the dead hand of Clausewitz had as tight a grip

on the opposing armies. This service at least he rendered his country. No army accepted his teaching
more blindly than the French—the more readily since
its leading soldiers had accepted him as the prophet of
Napoleon. That grip was strengthened because of the
grip which the Germans had obtained on their soil.
The desire to recover their lost territory henceforth
narrowed the thought and dominated the strategy of
the French leaders. The patriotic impulse had a personal reinforcement. Human nature ensured that
most generals would desire to see the war decided
when they were themselves in command: and nearly
all the leading generals, British as well as French,
were already holding commands on the Western
Front.

The common tendency was shown in the judgment,
as to future action, which Foch delivered when the
struggle at Ypres had drawn to its close. "The fate of
Europe has always been decided in Belgium"—hence
a "strong attack" here must pave the way for victory.
Although he would forget this dictum when he was
moved elsewhere, for the time his command-post and
Clausewitz coincided. "I remain faithful to pure theory—that which asserts that the destruction of the
enemy's military force will settle everything."

So far as the military issue was concerned this conclusion was so obvious that it is curious how few suspected there might be a catch in it. Neither Foch nor
his fellows paused to ask whether the idea was practicable in the existing conditions. The strongest part

of the enemy's forces lay in their front: crush this (they said) and the way to Berlin is clear. But how to crush it was a problem of which they took little account. Their solution was the customary device of "concentrating superior force at the decisive spot." It ignored the awkward fact that the more they concentrated their own forces the easier they made it for the enemy to concentrate against them. To make it worse for themselves they translated "force" in terms of numbers—the number of "bayonets."

Clausewitz, writing in the 1820's, had declared: "We may be sure that normally, in small as well as in great combats, an important superiority of numbers . . . will be sufficient to ensure the victory." "It is to be regarded as the fundamental idea, always to be aimed at." Even when he wrote, the musketry skill of the infantry of Frederick and Wolfe and Wellington, as well as the artillery methods of Napoleon, had provided exceptions to this rule. Yet it is easier to understand such a view being taken by a theorist in the dim dawn of the machine-age than to excuse its persistence after a century of mechanical development. The fact remains that, whether under Clausewitz's influence or from their inherent conservatism, the armies were tardy in grasping the possibilities of mechanical power and in appreciating its effect on their theories. Only with reluctance did they accept the new tools forced on them by civil progress, causing an immense and needless time-lag between the invention of these tools and their provision. The tale of the obstruction which each new weapon met from those who had most cause to welcome it—as exponents of superior force—would be incredible were it not established fact.

For a century the military manuals of Europe had continued to emphasize the decisive importance of physical shock, echoing Clausewitz's dictum: "the close combat, man to man, is plainly to be regarded as the real basis of combat." The French doctrine of 1914 fervently declared that the object of all attacks was "to charge the enemy with the bayonet in order to destroy him." (That idea would still remain in the British manuals until 1924.) Something might be claimed for it if the emphasis had been on the psychological effect of a close-quarter threat, but the time and attention devoted to bayonet-training showed that the bayonet-fight was regarded as a reality. Yet even in the eighteenth century a practical soldier like Guibert had remarked its rarity, while Jomini was but one of a number of witness of the Napoleonic battles who said that, except in villages and defiles, he had "never seen two forces cross bayonets." Half a century later Moltke would point out the fallacy of the French assertion that their victory at Solferino had been won by the bayonet. In 1870 their troops were to pay heavily against Prussian fire for this delusion among their leaders, yet Boguslawski records that in actual fact "bayonets were never crossed in open fight." But there is over two thousand years of experience to tell us that the only thing harder than getting a new idea into the military mind is to get an old one out.

Only in conditions where shock was a practical possibility could the theory of massing superior numbers be effective. It was difficult to adjust it to conditions where one man with a machine-gun might count for more than a score, or a hundred, or sometimes even a thousand, who were advancing upon him with the bayonet. As the capacity to make such an adjustment proved to be lacking, the formula of victory became merely a formula of futility—and death. The more ranks of attackers, the more swathes of dead: that was all.

It is easier to trace the origins of this misplaced trust in mass than to understand its persistence after sharp contact with reality. It was partly, perhaps, that for the generals the contact was at second-hand: and as experience multiplied the armies were also growing, with the result that the brains which controlled them became more remote from the nerve-tips which had the experience of direct contact. It was due partly, perhaps, to an uncritical attitude of mind: faith matters so much to a soldier in the stress of war that military training inculcates a habit of unquestioning obedience which in turn fosters an unquestioning acceptance of the prevailing doctrine. While fighting is a most practical test of theory, it is a small part of soldiering; and there is far more in soldiering that tends to make men the slaves of a theory. Moreover, the soldier must have faith in his power to defeat his enemy: that faith finds its fullest expression in the attack: hence to question, even on material grounds, the possibility of successful attack is a risk to faith. Doubt is unnerving save to philosophic minds: and armies

are not composed of philosophers, either at the top or
at the bottom. In no activity is optimism so necessary
to success, for it deals so largely with the unknown—
even unto death. The margin that separates optimism
from blind folly is narrow. There is no cause for surprise that soldiers so often overstep it and become the
victims of their faith.

This exploration of the foundations of military
psychology may help to explain why the military leaders remained confident of early victory despite continual disproof. In November 1914 Sir John French
asserted that all the hard fighting of the war was over.
In January 1915, he expressed the opinion that the
war itself would be over before June. In February
Joffre said that it would be over by July. In March
Haig felt sure that the Germans would be wanting
peace before the end of July; in July he declared that
they could not go on after the next January; a little
later, before his September offensive, he shortened the
predicted end, forecasting that it might come before
the winter arrived.

Kitchener was an exception to this habit, having
suggested in a flash of vision at the outset, that the
war might last three years. By June 1915, growing
weary of other soldiers' irrepressible optimism, he
complained: "Joffre and Sir John [French] told me in
November they were going to push the Germans back
over the frontier; they gave me the same assurances in
December, March and May. What have they done?
The attacks are very costly and end in nothing."

The effects of that false confidence were manifold.

Its immediate effects were twofold. On the one hand, it strengthened the soldiers' natural repugnance to any modification of their creed of concentration against the main enemy—to seeking a way round the trench-barrier that faced them across the whole breadth of the Western Front. On the other hand, it strengthened their natural resistance towards untried instruments—thus hindering the adoption of new means to overcome the trench-barrier. When the project of building the armoured trench-crossing machine that was christened the tank was submitted to the British Engineer-in-Chief in June 1915, he icily commented: "Before considering this proposal we should descend from the realms of imagination to solid facts." Eight months later, when the first tank demonstrated its powers before Kitchener he remarked: "A pretty mechanical toy"; adding that "the war would never be won by such machines."

The Stokes gun, a quick-firing trench-mortar, was submitted to the War Office as early as January 1915, and rejected. It was rejected afresh in March. The chance of overcoming the official barrier was due to the instant impression it made upon the new Minister of Munitions, Mr. Lloyd George, to whom it was demonstrated in June: as the Ministry of Munitions was then limited to the manufacture of weapons which the War Office had approved, he utilized a private donation from an Indian Maharajah to back the production of this mortar—which became the standard weapon of its kind.

The machine-gun itself, although it began to dominate the battlefield from the outset, was slow to be appreciated by the higher command. The German machine-guns had already paralysed the Allied attacks for months when an effort, in the spring of 1915, to increase the British strength in machine-guns was opposed by authority. On the proposal being referred to the army commanders Haig wrote in a minute, that "the machine-gun was a much overrated weapon and two per battalion were more than sufficient." At that time there were less than three hundred machine-guns in the whole British Army in France. Luckily a representative of the newly created Ministry of Munitions, Mr. (later Sir Eric) Geddes, went out to France to discover the Army's requirements. The head of the Machine-Gun School daringly said: "Twenty thousand." Geddes was more impressed by the foresight of this estimate than by the comments of General Headquarters on its absurdity. He sought the opinion of Kitchener, who conceded that four to a battalion might be useful, but any "above four may be counted as a luxury." Geddes showed this note to Mr. Lloyd George, who told him: "Take Kitchener's maximum; square it; multiply that result by two—and when you are in sight of that, double it again for good luck." This scale of manufacture anticipated the gradual rise in the military demands and the need for ample reserves.

The Ministry of Munitions was also quick to grasp the value of having a light machine-gun, easy to carry in an advance, and hastened the output of the Lewis gun—which had been rejected by the military authorities in 1912 on the ground that it was undesirable to multiply the types of arms, the rifle being considered adequate. By the end of the war the total output of machine-guns, heavy and light, had risen to 240,000: every battalion had thirty-two Lewis guns and, in action, usually had the support of at least half as many, and sometimes an equal number of, heavy machine-guns.

2. THE WESTERN FRONT

Throughout 1915, the French hurled themselves again and again on the entrenched front in the west—urged on by a desire to recover lost territory that was fixed by faith in a doctrine; and lured on by the mirage of early victory. Each time Joffre used a larger scale of munitions, and each time found that the defences had grown stronger in the interval. At the end of the year he had blunted the sword of France —so immense were the losses in the vain sacrifice. The total of casualties had risen from 850,000 in 1914 to nearly two and a half million. The British had likewise spent themselves in seconding his purpose: if their contribution here was still much smaller than that of their allies they had made it their main effort.

In the last weeks of 1914 Joffre attempted a great offensive in Flanders. To this he was encouraged by Foch's assurance, after the exhausting battle at Ypres, that "we are in perfect condition, both morally and materially, for attacking." Foch was sure that the Germans would have to fall back to the Meuse, at least, while Joffre was filled with the hope that he would "cut the enemy's communications with Germany." The offensive, however, proved a fiasco. The troops had no energy left and most of the executive commanders realized the folly of the attempt, with the result that each tended to wait upon his neighbours. The only effect was that produced on inter-allied relations.

A further combined offensive was arranged for March, but Joffre held his hand because the British had not complied with his desire that they should relieve one of his divisions at Ypres. Irritated by French jibes at his inactivity, Sir John French was impelled to deliver a single-handed attack at Neuve Chapelle on March 10th. This was entrusted to Haig's army, and in design foreshadowed subsequent trench-warfare methods although on a small scale. Forty-eight British battalions and three hundred and seventy-two guns were concentrated against a narrow sector held by less than two battalions of the enemy. Two cavalry corps waited behind ready to ride through the gap.

If the attackers' resources were smaller than in future attacks, the defenders' entrenchments were lighter—consisting only of a single line of breastwork covered by a thin barbed-wire entanglement. This was easily over-run in the first rush. But then "an astonishing paralysis crept over the whole movement." As was natural, the breach had not been cleanly cut at the two edges. The higher commanders were unwilling to let the advance continue until the flanks were cleared, and pushed in more troops for the purpose. Meantime, to quote the joint Official Historian, some "10,-000 men . . . lay, sat or stood uselessly in the mud, packed like salmon in the bridge pool at Galway, waiting patiently to go forward." Not until after 5 p. m. was the advance resumed, and then petered out in the dusk. During the seven hours since the breach had been made, the only force that barred the path numbered less than five hundred men, with three machine-guns. By next morning four times as many were on the spot, while a whole reserve division was hurrying thither. The renewed attack was a failure. On the third day Haig ordered the attack to be pushed "regardless of loss." And loss was the only result.

Meantime in Champagne the French had spent more for less promise. Here in February and March they lost 50,000 men in "nibbling" their way five hundred yards into the German defences: in his report Joffre claimed that the offensive "was none the less fecund in results." In April they sacrificed over 60,000 in an attack on the St. Mihiel salient which proved a complete fiasco.

On April 22nd the Germans retorted with a more effective salient-cut at the other end of the Western Front. During the previous weeks prisoners taken by the French near Ypres had disclosed that the Germans were preparing to discharge poison-gas from cylinders they had been placing in their trenches. On the 13th a deserter had even handed over a primitive gas-mask in proof of his statement. The local French commander was impressed, but he found that his superiors were incredulous: not only were his warnings ignored but he was rebuked for steps he had taken to forestall the danger. On the evening of the 22nd a strange mist crept forward from the German trenches against the left of the Ypres salient. Taken unawares and defenceless, the French troops here fled—save those who were already suffocated. The gas had swept a gap four miles wide in the front.

But the Germans failed to profit by the opportunity. When the idea of using gas had been propounded by Professor Haber, a distinguished chemist of Jewish origin, the higher command was slow to appreciate its potentialities. It was their scepticism rather than their scruples which limited Haber's facilities, so that he was forced to use cylinders instead of shells as the means of projection. The former depended on the chance of a favourable wind: the wind in Flanders was normally towards and not away from, the German trenches. Even when the German Command had decided to give a new weapon a trial their scepticism still prevailed to their own disadvantage. For Falkenhayn allotted no fresh reserves for the attack, and even refused the request for extra ammunition. Thereby the Germans incurred the odium of introducing a novel and horrifying weapon without adequate profit.

In the absence of reserves, the resistance of the Canadians on the flank of the breach and the arrival of English and Indian reinforcements saved the situation—although it did not save the cost. For a continued series of costly counter-attacks was made at Foch's optimistic urge to regain the lost ground, instead of straightening the line by withdrawing from a new con-stricted salient which was nothing but a shell-trap. When Smith-Dorrien protested, he was relieved of command by Sir John French. Foch continued to or-der attacks. But the exhausted French troops now nul-lified his orders by evasion—when zero-hour came "the French infantry did not leave its trenches." And after this the British Commander-in-Chief sanctioned the step for which he had sacked Smith-Dorrien—but only withdrew to a line which formed a smaller sal-ient. For the next month the Germans continued at-tacks against it which only ended when their ammuni-tion ran out. By that time the British had lost 60,000 men in the sentimental effort to hold what was strate-gically useless. For the next two years the British troops here would merely serve as an easy target for German artillery practice.

On May 9th Joffre's postponed offensive was launch-ed, near Arras. On the eve of it he predicted that it would be "the beginning of the end," and spoke of "getting to Namur and the war being over in three months." Foch was in direct charge and the plan marked a new stage in trench-warfare by definitely abandoning the idea of surprise in favour of a pro-longed bombardment, which lasted six days. A force of eighteen divisions with 1250 guns was concentrated against a twelve-mile sector held by four German divi-sions. The attack was soon held up except in the cen-tre, where Pétain's corps broke through to a depth of two miles. This success took the French Higher Command by surprise: before reserves could be brought up the gap had been closed. Nevertheless, the offensive was continued and the cavalry was told to be ready to pass through "at full gallop." All that happened was the gain of a few hundred yards at ever-growing cost. When the effort was at last suspended, the French losses had reached a total of 102,000. The British, attacking towards Aubers Ridge, had even less success and higher casualties in proportion.

If this offensive had made little impression on the German front, it left a deep impression on the French. One corps commander wrote that the troops had "lapsed into a gloomy sort of resignation." Another, when the French President visited the Arras sector entreated him to "put a stop to these local offensives; the instrument of victory is being broken in our hands." All the corps commanders who had shared in the offensive voiced the same opinion. Before it had been launched, Castelnau, the pre-war high priest of the offensive, had expressed his disbelief in any important result being obtainable, and after it he said that all attacks ought to be stopped until there was some chance of a real decision. Belief in such a possibility at an early date was now confined to Joffre and his entourage at Chantilly, the post most remote from the front—and so from reality. Even Foch had grown dubious by July.

Yet plans for a fresh offensive went forward—so strong is the binding power of the chain of command. Although it was reported to the President that "no single general, not even excepting Foch, has any more faith in an offensive proving successful," those generals were helpless to save their men from the fatal delusion of the general-in-chief. Their careers riveted their chains. Few were more honourable, according to their lights, than Castelnau; yet his doubts seem to have been silenced when Joffre put him on a level with Foch by making him commander of the centre group of armies and giving him the chief role in the projected September offensive. When Joffre held a conference of his army group commanders and discussed Kitchener's arguments in favour of standing on the defensive until British man-power and munitions had reached full tide, they agreed with him in dismissing it as "heresy." Then, inconsequently dropping the doctrinal argument, they declared: "Kitchener can pronounce at his ease, having no invaded provinces to liberate." Combined strategy was subordinated to simple sentiment.

For this futility on the Western Front much had been sacrificed beyond the immediate loss of life. By adherence to the theoretical ideal of destroying the main army of the main enemy, the allied chiefs would forfeit one actual point after another. They would encourage Bulgaria to join the enemy alliance, allow their own ally Serbia to be overrun, let slip the chance of probing Austria's weakness, and cause a great part of their own forces to be pinned down in the Near and Middle East throughout the whole war. During four years they pursued an ideal without seriously asking whether the conditions made it practicable. And at the end, as crowning irony, the issue would be decided

more by an economic means, the blockade, than by
any decisive victory in battle.

3. THE MEDITERRANEAN FRONT

An immediate cause of complication, if also of opportunity, lay in Turkey's entry into the war on
the German side. Want of British official sympathy
with the Young Turk revolution in 1909 had opened
the way for Germany, helped by Turkey's traditional
fear of Russia, to strengthen her influence at the expense of Turkey's traditional friendship with Britain.
German instructors had permeated the Turkish Army,
whose chief, Enver Pasha, had been military attaché
in Berlin. On July 27th, 1914, when war between Russia and Germany became a certainty, the Turkish
Government responding to earlier overtures, proposed a secret alliance with Germany against Russia.
The news of Britain's entry into the war, however,
caused so sharp a shock as to produce from Turkey the
astonishing offer of an alliance with Russia. But this
did not suit Russia's ambition—for the annexation of
Constantinople. And then, fatefully, the British Admiralty's action in taking over two Turkish battleships
which were being built in British shipyards produced
an outburst of wrath which tilted the scales. German
domination was further assured by the arrival of two
warships, the *Goben* and *Breslau*. These were allowed
to pass through the Dardanelles, and entry was barred
to the British. As Britain was slow to respond to growing provocation, at the end of October the German

admiral, with Enver's connivance, led the Turkish
fleet in a raid against the Russian ports in the Black
Sea. When the Turkish Grand Vizier made a belated
effort to evade responsibility, the German Embassy
warned him that it held in safe custody the Turk's
note of acquiescence, so "Pray cease to deny that the
Turkish Government has given the order to attack
Russia."

Under German dictation, and Enver's ambition for
martial glory, Turkey planned a December stroke
against the Russians in the Caucasus. In this wintry
venture she launched her only efficient force—and lost
it. Nor was she more fortunate in her next venture—to
cut the Suez Canal artery of Britain's power in the
East. This was easily repulsed in February.

But, for Germany, Turkey's entry provided a valu-
able distraction to the forces of the British Empire, as
well as of the Russian. And it bolted the Black Sea
back-gate by which Russia and potential millions of
men might have been furnished with adequate munitions.

Turkey's participation in the war provided the
Allies with an alternative idea for their strategy—that
of lopping off Germany's "limbs" before attacking the
trunk. Its advocates—who became known as "Eastern," in contrast to the "Western" school—declared
that it was folly to strike where the enemy were strongest. They argued that the enemy alliance should be
viewed as a whole, pointing out that a stroke in some
some other theatre of war was merely the modern form
of the classic method of attack on an enemy's strategic

flank. Such an operation would accord with the traditional amphibious strategy of Britain, enabling her to exploit the hitherto neglected advantages of sea-power.

At the end of August the growing signs of Turkey's hostility, combined with an offer of assistance from Greece, had prompted Churchill to discuss with Kitchener the idea of forcing the Dardanelles. Three weeks after Turkey's entry into the war, he raised it afresh at the first meeting of the new War Council, pointing out that such an attack was the ideal way of forestalling danger to Egypt. But troops were lacking, and eyes were focused on the Western Front, also, the Greek king had changed his mind. The project was shelved.

In December the evidence of Turkish designs against Egypt, combined with the arrival there of the Australian and New Zealand Expeditionary Force, led Kitchener to regard with favour a scheme for a diversion against the Turkish communications by a landing in Ayas Bay near Alexandretta—at the "corner" between Asia Minor and Syria—where the solitary railway which linked Turkey with her Empire passed close to the sea. This scheme was devised by a young temporary second lieutenant of three months service who later became famous as Lawrence of Arabia: he held that such a landing would have "handed over Syria and Mespot to their native (Arab) troops then all in their home stations . . . and automatically established local governments there: and then attracted to Ayas the whole bulk of the *real* Turkish armies—to fritter itself against the Arabs, not against us: and that would have been the moment for the Dardanelles naval effort." Kitchener contemplated applying the plan as soon as the Dominion troops were ready.

By this time the deadlock in France had become increasingly clear except to the commanders on the spot. And these now unwittingly strengthened the case for an alternative move by the assurance which Sir John French, with Joffre's concurrence, gave the Government on December 28th—that "the French had no fears regarding their ability to deal with any possible break that might occur in the Franco-British line, and that they now believed such a contingency to be more than ever remote."

In a paper of December 29th, 1914, Lieut.-Colonel Maurice Hankey, the Secretary of the War Council, had emphasized the deadlock in the West. While urging the development of new mechanical and armoured devices to force a passage through the wire entanglements and trenches, he suggested that in the prevailing conditions Germany could be struck more effectively through her allies. Hence he proposed that the first three of the newly raised "Kitchener" Army Corps should be used for an attack on Constantinople with the combined aim of knocking Turkey out of the war, bringing the weight of the Balkan countries into the Allied scales, and opening a line of supply for Russia.

At the same time Mr. Lloyd George drafted a paper in which he urged that Britain would soon have a new force of at least half a million ready for service; that this addition was unlikely to "make any real differ-

ence" to the unmistakable "stalemate" in France; that
as the French were confident of being able to hold the
front with their present forces the bulk of the new
British forces should be used to develop an alternative
move. He suggested that this should be "an attack upon Austria, in conjunction with the Serbians, the Roumanians and the Greeks." It would come against "her
most vulnerable frontier." At the same time, as Turkish forces were now moving down towards the Egyp-
tian frontier, a smaller "force of 100,000 should be
landed in Syria to cut them off," by getting astride
their sole, and seacoast, line of railway communication.

If Lloyd George's main suggestion did not take full
account of the difficulties of sending up or supplying
so large an army "through Salonika or . . . the Dalma-
tian coast," it did not pretend to be more than a scheme
for technical examination and adjustment. Moreover,
his concluding remarks emphasized the need of
prompt and thorough study, saying prophetically:
"Expeditions decided upon and organized with insufficient care and preparation generally end disastrous-
ly."

It is significant that, on New Year's day also, Galliéni proposed to the French Government a similar
landing in Salonika, as a starting point for a march on
Constantinople with an army strong enough to encourage Greece and Bulgaria to join in it. The capture
of Constantinople would be followed by an advance
up the Danube, an easier line of supply than from

Salonika, to develop an attack on Austria in conjunction with the Roumanians. Franchet d'Esperey had already made similar proposals. And after a few more months of vain effort other eminent French soldiers, including Castelnau, came to share these views—although few cared to voice them in the hearing of Joffre.

It may seem curious that more British generals did not incline the same way—for such a strategy was in accord with Britain's historic practice. It had, indeed, been elevated into a theory by the Tory party in the eighteenth century. Yet now, ironically, the most rooted "Westerners" both within and without the Army were staunch Conservatives—who might have been horrified if they had realized that they were violating the Tory tradition! The first cause was that the British Army, being late to take up the study of war seriously, had gone to Continental sources for its ideas. The second cause was that in August 1914 almost all the leading British soldiers had gone to France: and their views henceforth were bounded by their own immediate horizon.

Kitchener was an exception. On January 2nd, 1915, he wrote to Sir John French:

"I suppose we must now recognize that the French Army cannot make a sufficient break through the German lines of defence to . . . bring about the retreat of the German forces from Northern France. If that is so, then the German lines in France may be looked upon as a fortress that cannot be carried by assault, and also

cannot be completely invested—with the result that
the lines can only be held by an investing force, while
operations proceed elsewhere."

The minds of Hankey, Lloyd George, Churchill,
and Kitchener—four powerful influences—were all
moving in the same direction, if not to the same point.
And now, just as there was a chance of proper investigation, an accident of fate gave the movement a twist.
It took the form of an appeal from Russia for a demonstration to relieve the Turkish pressure on her forces
in the Caucasus. The appeal had scarcely arrived before the threat had collapsed; but before this was
known great events had been set in train. Having no
troops yet available, Kitchener suggested that a naval
demonstration against the Dardanelles might help.
Churchill seized upon the suggestion and amplified it
through a hint from Fisher, the First Sea Lord, that
old battleships might be used to force the Dardanelles.
He wired to Carden, the admiral on the spot: "Do you
consider the forcing of the Straits by ships alone a
practicable operation?" The admiral replied that it
might be done by methodical operations. He was
asked to elaborate his views. Meantime the discussion
on an alternative theatre for the New Armies continued, and Kitchener inclined towards the Dardanelles,
with the Alexandretta landing as a preliminary move.

This threat to his own plans brought Sir John
French back in haste to see the War Council. Despite
his remarkable admission that complete success in the
West was "not probable," and that, if it proved impossible to break through, an attack on Austria would

be a desirable alternative, he gained permission to pursue the improbability. This was an inevitable check to the prospect of diverting troops to the Mediterranean.

The War Council then turned to the next business: Churchill laid before them Admiral Carden's plan. Here was the prospect of a success without finding troops, and apparently with little to be lost if the venture failed. The War Council jumped at it, all the more readily because the Balkan scales were hovering uncertainly and policy had urgent need of some early military success to aid it. So the Admiralty was instructed "to prepare for a naval expedition in February, to bombard and take the Gallipoli peninsula, with Constantinople as its objective." The haziness implicit in the suggestion that ships were to "take" an area of land capped the fateful course of this meeting on January 13th.

A week later Churchill suggested that, as a safeguard, the Alexandretta landing might coincide with the naval attack on the Dardanelles. Kitchener replied that no troops could be spared for this at present. Then at the War Council meeting on the 28th it was reported that the Committee which had been studying the problem of an alternative theatre for the New Armies were in favour of Salonika, emphasizing the importance of supporting Serbia. This coincided with an offer from Greece to join forces with Serbia if four British or French divisions were sent. Kitchener reiterated that no troops could yet be spared. There were, in fact, four trained divisions now available in

England. But French was pressing for their despatch to France, Joffre was pressing him, and Kitchener was more sensitive to the wishes of the French than to the value of time. From this time on the allied headquarters in France were united in opposing any plan that might take away even a fraction of the troops dedicated to the dream of early victory in the West. Their opposition delayed, and finally strangled, the alternative schemes.

On February 9th, the War Council heard ominous news of Bulgaria's inclination towards the German side. The obvious danger revived the Salonika project; Kitchener was led to offer the 29th Division and the French agreed to send a division. But the tardy offer was too small to satisfy Greece in taking the risk of marching to Serbia's aid. The knowledge that troops were available now caused the Government to take the decision that they should be utilized to support the Dardanelles attempt in case of necessity. Even now, however, under pressure from Joffre, Kitchener delayed their despatch. As the Official History remarks: "It would seem that this last remaining Regular division was being regarded by French G.H.Q. as a symbol of Britain's future attitude with regard to the Western Front."

Meanwhile the naval attack on the Dardanelles went forward, and no one suggested that it might be withheld until a combined stroke could be delivered by surprise. On February 19th the bombardment of the outer forts began; after they had been evacuated by the Turks demolition parties were landed. Two months later thousands of men were to be sacrificed in reoccupying the spot of land where this handful of marines moved freely.

The echoes of this bombardment travelled far, and had a remarkable effect. The Turkish Government made ready to abandon Constantinople. The Germans expected a revolt against Enver and their own abandonment by Turkey, who could not carry on the war once Constantinople, their only munition source, was lost. Bulgaria repented her inclination towards the German side. Italy and Greece made fresh moves towards joining the other side.

The naval advance was continued, but in a rather desultory way against the intermediate defences. Under the spur of a telegram from the Admiralty, a general fleet attack was launched on March 18th—by Admiral de Robeck, as Carden had gone sick. In the interval the Turks had laid a fresh row of mines in a bay where the Allied fleet had been accustomed to manœuvre during earlier bombardments. The forts had been practically silenced, and the minesweepers sent in to clear the main passage, when a French battleship struck this unsuspected row of mines and sank in less than two minutes with nearly all her crew. Two hours later a couple of British battleships struck it almost simultaneously, and were badly damaged. Fear of the unknown prompted de Robeck to order a general retirement immediately. Although one of the damaged ships had sunk, as well as another sent to her aid, the British loss of life was only sixty-one men. The Admiralty telegraphed that five more battleships were being sent out and—that "it was important not . . . to encourage the enemy by an apparent suspension of the operations."

Yet de Robeck now decided that he "could not get through" without the help of the army—and in the months that followed made no further attempt to do so, despite much prompting. Sir Ian Hamilton had already arrived on the scene, as commander of the troops who were being sent out, and onto his shoulders de Robeck unloaded the burden.

At the moment that de Robeck had signalled the order for a hasty retirement, the Turkish defenders of the Straits were on the verge of collapse. They had no reserve of mines, most of their ammunition had been expended, and the gun-crews were demoralized. German as well as Turkish officers felt they had little hope of resisting any renewal of the naval attack.

The military attack began under heavy handicaps —the worst being lack of organization. At the War Office not a single preparatory step had been taken. When Hamilton was hurried out to the Dardanelles at a day's notice, the sum of his information comprised a pre-war handbook on the Turkish Army, a pre-war report on the forts, and a map which proved inaccurate. He found, moreover, that his troops had been so chaotically distributed in their transports that they had to be sent to Alexandria for redistribution, thus entailing several weeks further delay.

Hitherto, Turkish lethargy, increased by a fatalistic belief that they could not resist a serious attack, had forfeited the value of the ample warning that the Brit-

ish had given them. The Turkish Staff History frank-
ly confesses that "up to February 25th it would have
been possible to effect a landing successfully at any
point on the peninsula, and the capture of the Straits
by land troops would have been comparatively easy."
Not until March 25th did Enver create a proper force
and place it under the German general Liman von
Sanders: who, after a hurried survey, exclaimed: "If
the English will only leave me alone for eight days."
They gave him a month's grace. When the naval attack had begun there were only two Turkish divisions
present to guard the whole area. By the time Hamilton was able to attempt a landing, they had risen to six
—and he had only five divisions (75,000 men against
84,000) for this hazardous landing on a hostile shore.

Yet by his amphibious advantage and his plan he
regained the effect of surprise. The landing was made
on April 25th—by the 29th Division at five points near
Cape Helles at the top of the peninsula; by the Australian and New Zealand Corps near Gaba Tepe, fifteen
miles up the outer or Aegean coast. The remaining
British division sailed north as if to land at the neck of
the peninsula, near Bulair, while the French division,
as a diversion made a temporary landing on the Asiatic
shore. The wideness of the menace, and the dispersion
of the landing places, mystified the enemy so completely that forty-eight hours passed before they began to
concentrate their forces: their reserves had been
rushed north to Bulair, leaving only one division to
defend the peninsula itself.

The opportunity so created went begging. Machine-guns and submerged wire had made V and W Beaches a death-trap for the original landing parties: yet it was here that the commander of the 29th Division concentrated his efforts. Meantime the almost unopposed attackers at the other beaches remained inert, although by a short advance they could easily have cut off the defenders of V and W, whom they greatly outnumbered. At Y the landing force, which was here in the enemy's rear, sat still all day although it alone was equal in strength to the whole of the Turkish forces in the south of the peninsula. At Gaba Tepe the Australians gained an almost bloodless lodgment, thanks to the wisdom of landing before daybreak: and then had a superiority of sixteen to one over the defence. But the country was rough, the troops raw, and the advance became ragged. Thus the opportunity was missed and from the afternoon onwards the Australians suffered a series of counter-attacks. That night they were in such a state that their commander was on the verge of re-embarking them when Hamilton intervened, sending the message: "Now you have only to dig, dig, dig, until you are safe."

The opportunity lost could not be regained either here or at Helles. The Turks held the commanding heights and were able to bring up their reserves. The energy of the attackers was spent, and when they renewed their efforts against an entrenched enemy their scanty artillery lacked the ammunition to make an impression: Ian Hamilton was allowed but a fraction of the quantity of shells that were being expended for nothing on the Western Front. Thus stagnation settled in. The British troops could not advance and national prestige forbade their withdrawal. A driblet of two more divisions was sent too late.

Two months passed before the Government, under Churchill's vehement prompting, decided to raise Hamilton's force to a total of a dozen divisions. By the time these reinforcements arrived the Turkish strength had also risen, to fifteen divisions. The root cause of this fatal hesitation was the opposition, open and un·derground, of the French and British commanders on the Western Front, who begrudged every man diverted from the services of the main offensive there. Despite the intention of using the New Armies in an alternative theatre, no less than sixteen new divisions were added between May and September to the twenty-one in France, compared with five sent to Gallipoli.

For his second attempt Ian Hamilton planned a double stroke—a reinforced blow from "Anzac" (Gaba Tepe) and a new landing at Suvla Bay, a few miles to the north. By this he hoped to cut astride the peninsula and secure the heights that commanded the Straits. Once more, with the help of sea-borne mobility, he deceived the enemy command only to be baffled by the combination of incapable commanders and raw troops on his side. His appeal that he might be given some of the younger generals who had proved themselves in France had been refused, and he had to take what was available under the restrictions of "Army List seniority." The venture was launched on August 6th.

At Anzac the enemy's forward posts were rushed by surprise in the dark, and two columns were then passed through, with a clear if rugged path ahead of them. They came close to gaining the heights only to be baulked by a combination of time-wasting mistakes and mischances. One column chose to halt a quarter of a mile short of the crest, which was then held by only twenty Turks: by the time it had finished breakfast the ridge was "bristling with rifles." The other column became tangled up with itself and came to a full stop, far short of its objective, when "apart from occasional sniping, all opposition had ceased." The caution of the commanders was accentuated by the exhaustion of the troops—many of them unfit—who had been weighed down with heavy loads.

At Suvla 20,000 men were safely landed on an almost unguarded part of the coast and "were well-placed to outflank the main Turkish forces already hotly engaged at Anzac." For thirty-six hours their path was barred by a detachment of little more than a thousand Turks, who were without any machine-guns. There were no enemy reserves within a thirty-mile radius. But the British frittered away the hours while opportunity yawned on a deserted ridge. On arrival in Suvla Bay the Corps Commander, Stopford, settled down to sleep on board without sending anyone ashore or wondering why no news came from the shore. On the afternoon of the 8th he was still on board: nor had he once gone ashore to see even his divisional commanders—instead, he had sent them congratulatory messages. In this example of complacent inertia his subordinates found an excuse, if not a justification, for their own. Their dominant thought was to consolidate, not to push on. The naval arrangements also broke down, not least in keeping the Commander-in-Chief prisoner at his headquarters on the isle of Imbros when he had awoken to the fact that his personal intervention was needed.

Meantime, the Turkish reserves were at last hurrying to the scene. When their commander had shown hesitation, "Limon von Sanders, more ruthless than Sir Ian Hamilton," had sacked him on the spot, putting in his place Mustapha Kemal, who had saved the situation at Anzac in April. Now by his fierce energy he turned the scales again—with his opponents' help. When the British attack at last developed on the 9th under Hamilton's gentler spur, the odds were more level, and the effort failed. Its renewals did little more than pile up the casualty list.

The British were once more left hanging onto narrow footholds and, with the onset of the autumn rains, their trials increased. The Government had lost faith and were anxious to withdraw, especially as they had fresh burdens on their hands. Their decision was delayed by fear of the moral effect, and also of the loss that might be suffered in the process of evacuation—the General Staff estimate was 50,000 casualties. But they were still more apprehensive of staying there and when Ian Hamilton declared in favour of continuing—in which course he still had confidence—he was replaced by Sir Charles Munro, commander of an army in France.

Asked to report on the situation, Munro provided an example of prompt decision. While he visited Anzac, Suvla, and Helles in a single morning, without going further than the beach, his Chief of Staff, staying on board ship, was already drafting the recommendation for evacuation. Kitchener at first refused to sanction the withdrawal and himself hurried out to investigate. But the adverse gusts of opinion at home were now developing into a gale and after his revived proposal for a fresh landing near Alexandretta had been vetoed by the War Committee, he reluctantly veered round and consented to evacuation. The withdrawal of the troops was carried out from Suvla and Anzac on the night of December 18th, and from Helles on that of January 8th.

Not a single man had lost his life. As the last lighters quitted the derelict piers of Helles with the last British troops who would set foot on the peninsula until after the war, the dark sky was suddenly reddened with the glare of blazing dumps and stabbed with Turkish rockets soaring skyward in alarm. The German commanders might regret the lost opportunity, but the Turkish soldiers showed nothing but relief. Thus ended a sound and farsighted venture which had been wrecked by a chain of errors hardly to be rivalled even in British history.

What its success would have meant at the minimum to the Franco-British cause is best shown in the testimony of the directing head of the Germanic alliance. For it was Falkenhayn's verdict that "If the straits between the Mediterranean and the Black Sea were not permanently closed to Entent traffic, all hopes of a successful issue of the war would be very seriously diminished. Russia would have been freed from her significant isolation which . . . offered a safer guarantee than military success . . . that the forces of this Titan would eventually and automatically be crippled." And Hoffmann, the guiding brain of the German campaign against Russia declared that its success depended on keeping "the Dardanelles firmly closed."

Even though it failed, the Gallipoli expedition had produced important effects. For by its threat it had upset the whole war plan of the Germans for 1915. Falkenhayn had intended to make another bid for victory in the west, and, like Joffre, had an unquenchable belief in its prospects. His plans were upset by the cracks which began to appear in the Austrian defences. The menace to Austria, quivering under the pressure from Russia and Serbia, became obvious when the Dardanelles attack opened. Falkenhayn felt that he must cut out the Serbian ulcer from Austria's side before it was swollen by Allied reinforcements. But before he could even do this the Russians must be pushed back to a safe distance.

It was ironical that Joffre and French, who had striven so hard to thwart the Gallipoli expedition, should have been saved by that starveling campaign from the danger of meeting a German onslaught in the west: that they should have owed the chance of pursuing their dream of victory to the very move whose value they had failed to appreciate, even as a distraction to the enemy's concentration.

4. THE EASTERN FRONT

Falkenhayn suffered distraction from internal as well as external opponents. Throughout 1915 he was engaged in ceaseless struggle with the leaders on the Eastern Front, Conrad and Hindenburg—behind whom was the dominating mind of Ludendorff. Their desire was to concentrate on crushing the Russian armies, on winning a decisive victory on the front where they were in charge. The outcome was a conflict of wills damaging to the German strategy.

At the end of 1914 Falkenhayn had formed a Tenth Army from new reserves: this he intended to be his striking force in France. But Hindenburg clamoured for it, and when refused he appealed to the Kaiser, urging Falkenhayn's dismissal. He had taken the precaution to gain the support of the Kaiserin and the Chancellor. The Kaiser compromised by retaining Falkenhayn in office with diminished powers and consoling Hindenburg with the gift of the Tenth Army. It was used in February for a stroke from East Prussia over snow-buried roads and frozen swamps: this broke the front and led to the capture of 90,000 men near the Masurian Lakes but failed in its bigger aims.

Meantime the Russians from Southern Poland were pushing back the Austrians. On March 23rd the long-invested fortress of Przemysl at last fell, with 120,000 men, into the Russians' hands. They now gained the passes of the Carpathians, threatening to pour into the plains of Hungary.

Falkenhayn had been building up a fresh striking force in France—and plans had been studied which would not be fulfilled until 1918. Then the menace of the British attack on the Dardanelles, and its effect on the Balkan countries, drove Falkenhayn to the conclu sion that he "must carry out the Serbian campaign be fore the great offensive he had planned in the west.' (It is interesting to note that his thought was moving just as Lloyd George had forecast at a meeting of the War Council on February 19th—a forecast on which Kitchener had cast doubt.) The need was the more pressing because of Italy's imminent entry into the war. Now came the grave news of the crisis in the Car-pathians. Falkenhayn decided that he must help the Austrians to drive back the Russians before even cut-ting a route to Turkey through Serbia.

He accepted Conrad's plan for a flank stroke on the north of the Carpathians in the Gorlice-Tarnow sec-tor. For this purpose he brought the newly formed Eleventh Army from the west, placing it, together with an Austrian army, under the command of Mack-ensen—who was given as his Chief of Staff, and brain, Colonel Seeckt, the man who was to rebuild the Ger-man Army after the war. Fourteen divisions with 1000 guns were concentrated on a quiet sector held by six Russian divisions. And Seeckt introduced a method of maintaining the momentum of an advance—by back· ing up success instead of trying to redeem local checks —which foreshadowed the famous "infiltration" meth-od of 1918.

The thrust, on May 3rd, easily pierced the shallow

Russian front. As the assailants swept forward, "loam-grey figures jumped up and ran back, weaponless, in grey fur caps and fluttering, unbuttoned greatcoats. Soon there was not one of them remaining. Like a flock of sheep they fled in wild confusion." The exploitation was rapid, rolling up the whole Russian line along the Carpathians. By the 14th an eighty-mile advance, to the San, had been achieved.

Falkenhayn now wished to carry out his stroke against Serbia. But for this he needed the help of Bulgaria, and she withheld her decision while waiting to see if the British attack on the Dardanelles succeeded. This indefiniteness, coupled with the fact that the British did not look like gaining an early success, led Falkenhayn to pursue his own success against the Russians. His armies broke through the new-knit front and the Russian armies, starved of munitions, relapsed into a prolonged retreat, abandoning a four-hundred mile stretch of territory and leaving 400,000 prisoners in the enemy's hands. But with such masses as the attackers were themselves employing, the rate of advance was too slow to overtake and round up the bulk of the retreating armies. And the Russians from their vaster resources would not be long in making good their lost man-power.

Falkenhayn's continued anxiety about his Austrian allies led him to yield to Seeckt's insistence and continue the offensive. This time it was directed northward to cut off the Russian forces in the Polish salient with the aid of a converging attack from East Prussia. Ludendorff disliked the plan: the Russians might be squeezed by the closing in of the two wings but their retreat would not be cut off. He urged again his favourite idea of a wide enveloping manœuvre round the north by Vilna against the Russians' rear. Falkenhayn resisted this project, fearing that it would call for more troops and draw him like Napoleon too deep into Russia. The Kaiser this time supported him and the "shears" plan was adopted instead of the "net." The Russians justified Ludendorff's expectation, extricating themselves from the Polish salient, although by the middle of August their loss in prisoners had risen to three-quarters of a million.

Falkenhayn now decided to break off his general offensive on the Eastern Front and turn against Serbia— as the failure of the second British effort as the Dardanelles had encouraged Bulgaria to jump down from the fence on Germany's side.

But, partly in the hope of placating his personal opponents, he gave Ludendorff belated permission to try his Vilna stroke with such resources as he had. This opened promisingly on September 9th, but the Russians had been allowed to draw back too far, and they were able to meet and frustrate the threat. Conrad, too, had taken the opportunity of attempting another "Gorlice" on his own. It was a dismal failure and through unwise persistence he sacrificed nearly quarter of a million men without effect—save to Austria's detriment.

By October the Russian armies, after their months-long ordeal were safely halted on a straightened line from Riga on the Baltic to Czernowitz on the Rou·

manian frontier. Although they had escaped destruction they had been badly lamed and would never
again be a direct menace to Germany. Their defeats
were due above all, to want of munitions. Even at the
end of 1914 the Chief of Staff of the Russian field
armies had been writing to the War Minister that the
shortage of ammunition was "a nightmare" and that
"many of the men are without boots and have frost-
bitten feet. . . . They say: 'Why should we perish of
hunger and cold, without boots; the artillery is silent,
and we are killed like partridges. The Germans are
better off. Let us go.'" Yet at this time, and for long
after, France and Britain were still talking confidently
of the "Russian steam-roller." Indeed, when Joffre
heard that the British Government was anxious lest
Russia might collapse he exclaimed that they were
"mad," and silenced his own Government's inclination to help the Dardanelles move by declaring: "If
you take away one single man that I can use on my
front *I will resign.*" In May the Russian Chief of Staff
reported: "From all armies the cry goes up: Give us
cartridges!" In June it was reported that "150,000 are
without rifles," that owing to the lack of shells "the
enemy can inflict loss unpunished," and that the fighting was "pure murder."

For this, inevitably, the commanders in the west
were culpable, through their opposition to the Dardanelles expedition. Nor had Joffre and French relieved
the strain by their efforts in the west—for the summer
offensive there had done no more than draw off two
German divisions from the east, at a time when Fal-

kenhayn could spare them without inconvenience. And now another ally was to suffer still worse for this obsession.

5. SERBIA OVERRUN

Austria's attempted invasion of Serbia in August and September, and again in November 1914, had been brusquely repulsed by Serbian counter-strokes. The Serbian infantry were born fighters, but the lack of modern equipment hampered them in following up their successes. Throughout the first nine months of 1915 Serbia stood idle.

One of the most astonishing "blind spots" in French and British strategy was its failure to see the importance of Serbia as an irritation, and consequent distraction to the Austro-German alliance in a most sensitive region. The injury which the "Spanish ulcer" inflicted on the Napoleonic forces might now have been repeated by the "Serbian ulcer" in sapping the Teutonic strength. To maintain the irritation, quality rather than quantity of aid was needed from Serbia's allies—the provision of technical troops and material. But the obsession with "mass" interfered. Because of this theory, and, more justifiably, because of the difficulty of communications unless the Danube route was opened, the military leaders in the west were unwilling to send large forces: they could see no mean between this and sending practically nothing. By their neglect they allowed the enemy to operate on the Serbian ulcer, with results that would cause cumulative trouble to themselves.

On October 6th, 1915, the Austro-German striking force under Mackensen crossed the Danube. A week later the Bulgarian armies struck westward into Southern Serbia across the defenders rear. Sturdy resistance and the natural difficulty of the mountainous country delayed the invaders, thwarting their efforts to cut off the Serbians. But the Bulgarians advance had cut the line of retreat to, or help from, Salonika. Isolated and hard-pressed, the Serbians were driven to retreat west through Albania. Those who survived the hardships of this mid-winter retreat over the mountains were conveyed to the island of Corfu. In the spring of 1916, after being reorganized and re-equipped, they joined the forces of the Entente at Salonika.

The conquest of Serbia relieved Austria of danger on her southern frontier, opened communication with Turkey, and gave Germany control over a huge central belt from the North Sea and the Baltic to the Tigris.

Moreover by digging themselves in at Salonika the Allies had dug a strategic sump-pit for themselves: for three years it would be a drain on their military resources although in the end it would overflow and wash away—one of the props of the Central Powers. In late September the imminence if a combined Austro-German attack on Serbia with Bulgaria's assistance had become clear to the British and French Governments. Sir Edward Grey declared in the House of Commons: "We are prepared to give our friends in the Balkans all the support in our power . . . without reserve and without qualification." But Joffre and French would still impose fresh qualifications before parting with any of their reserves. Although Joffre had previously promised to spare some for the Mediterranean after his September offensive, if it failed, now that it had failed he tried to wriggle out of his promise. Meantime one British and one French division were taken from Gallipoli and sent to Salonika, arriving on October 5th. Even then they were slow to advance. Difficulties had arisen with Greece who was now thoroughly suspicious of the Entente policy and impressed by the German successes. The British Government thereupon took the attitude that they had only sent troops to enable Greece to fulfil her obligations to Serbia, and at first refused to let their troops advance. Joffre now turned a somersault, much to the astonishment of the British Command, and urged the necessity of sending more troops to Salonika.

At the end of October, the French relief force under Sarrail, now reinforced by two more divisions, pressed up the Vardar across the Serbian frontier—only to find that the Bulgarian wedge had separated it from the Serbians. Too late to be of service, it was itself endangered when the Bulgarians turned upon it, and early in December fell back on Salonika. The British, now raised to five divisions, helped in covering the retreat.

On military grounds the evacuation of Salonika was vigorously urged by Robertson, the new head of the British General Staff, but the French were now no less strongly in favour of staying; their influence, backed by political reasons, settled the issue. The forces were swollen by the arrival of Italian and Russian contingents as well as by the rebuilt Serbian Army. But Robertson, foiled of his desire to withdraw, thereafter steadily withheld the means necessary to enable the British contingent to play its part adequately in an offensive there. Apart from the capture of Monastir in November 1916 and an abortive attack in April 1917, the ill-mixed army in Macedonia, which rose to half a million men, made no serious offensive until the autumn of 1918. On their side the Germans were content to leave it in peace, under guard of the Bulgarians. With pointed sarcasm they termed Salonika their "largest internment camp."

6. THE AUTUMN OFFENSIVE IN THE WEST

On September 25th, Joffre had launched in France the great offensive for which so much had been sacrificed. This, too, made its not inconsiderable addition to the bill. Joffre's plan was to strike a two-handed blow against the sides of the huge salient formed by the German line in Northern France. Castelnau's army was to strike in Champagne; Foch was to strike near Arras with the British co-operating on his left, towards Loos. A break-through in these two sectors was to be followed by a general advance which "would compel the Germans to retreat beyond the Meuse and possibly end the war." The original idea was that Foch's should be the principal blow.

When Joffre sent his draft plan to the British in June, Haig, whose army would have to carry it out, objected that their supply of heavy guns and shells was still inadequate to justify such an ambitious offensive. He also declared that the proposed sector was not a favourable one for attack. But Joffre, from his remote headquarters, brushed these objections aside, declaring that it was "particularly favourable ground." Sir John French then thought to evade the difficulty by co-operating with artillery fire alone. Henry Wilson, discovering his chief's intention, betrayed it to the French headquarters who thereupon appealed to Kitchener, throwing out alarming hints that unless the British gave full help Joffre would be displaced and the French politicians would make peace. Kitchener thereupon insisted that French must do his utmost.

As he had so often expressed his view that the Western Front was impregnable, Kitchener's reversal of attitude was curious. One factor was apparently his thought—if hardly a reasoned thought—that it might aid the Russians, then staggering under repeated blows. Another factor is suggested by the disclosure in the Official History that he "anticipated a call" to take supreme command of the Allied Forces when Britain's full strength was in the field. If he opposed the French appeal now that call would become unlikely.

The offensive was finally fixed for September 25th, and at a conference beforehand Joffre declared that the simultaneous attacks in two sectors were "a certain guarantee of success" and that he was "confident of a great and possibly complete victory." The cavalry were moved up with orders to "make a relentless pursuit without waiting for the infantry, and with the frontier as their objective." Joffre's plan definitely sacrificed surprise to the destruction of the enemy's defences, the assault being preceded by a bombardment lasting four days. Its chances were improved by Falkenhayn who disbelieved the abundant warnings he had received and refused to reinforce the threatened sectors. Only two hours before the attack opened he told the Kaiser that the French were not in a condition to attack. If he thus helped the French to an opening success this had a delusive effect because the local German commanders drew back their main strength to their second position, a method which foreshadowed the "elastic" defence of 1918.

As a result the French, in Champagne, after overrunning the first position, failed to make any real impression on the second. Yet for three days they vainly hurled themselves against it, until the loss was at last curtailed by Pétain suspending his attack in disregard of higher orders. Joffre pushed the harder here, because in the final plan he had made it his main stroke, alloting it thirty-four divisions. This gave the troops here a superiority of five to one over the enemy, compared with three to one in the attack near Arras. The reduction of Foch's effort reacted unfavourably on the British attack. Foch's troops made little progress; the fighting commanders, having lost faith in his dreams through prolonged experience, seem to have nullified his vehement orders by gentle

evasion. Contrasting the feeble results obtained near
Arras with the delusive air of victory in Champagne,
Joffre in the second day temporarily stopped the attack, while telling Foch to "take care to avoid giving
the British the impression that we are leaving them to
attack alone."

The British offensive was delivered at 6-30 a.m., six
hours before Foch's. Counting on Sir John French's
reserve of three divisions to back him up, Haig
launched all his six divisions in the first assault—
against four German regiments. This gave him a superiority of seven to one in troops, although he had
less than half as many heavy guns to the mile as the
French. Despite his earlier doubts, his optimism had
grown as the time drew nearer, and so great became
his expectations from the coming blow that he privately conveyed a warning against the tendency in
England to count on the campaign lasting through
the winter. The newspapers, he considered, were underrating the Germans' rate of exhaustion.

Haig's hopes for his own success had been raised by
the possibility of using cloud-gas. But the wind played
him false, and the effect was worsened because one of
the divisional commanders had overruled his gas expert's objection by the order that "the programme
must be carried out whatever the conditions"—with
the result that he gassed his own men. Nevertheless,
it was partially effective on the right, and here the
15th Division almost broke through—causing a panic
in the German command. Whatever chance there was
of exploiting this narrow penetration vanished be-

cause Sir John French, disregarding Haig's remonstrances, had kept the only reserves sixteen miles in rear. Also he was late in handing them over to Haig and their arrival was further delayed by muddled traffic arrangements. As the Official History remarks: "It was like trying to push the Lord Mayor's procession through the streets of London, without clearing the route and holding up the traffic." The ordeal was all the worse since they were raw divisions, and it was accentuated by Haig's eagerness to retrieve the lost time. They pushed on across country in the dark and rain: next morning, tired, hungry, and confused, they were launched without effective artillery support against defences which had now been cemented and strengthened. The attack broke down and the survivors broke back.

German counter-attacks and bad weather imposed a long delay. Yet Joffre, French and Haig were united now in a determination to continue the offensive. It was eventually renewed on all three sectors on different dates, the British last, on October 13th. The Official History comments on its result that it "had not improved the general situation in any way and had brought nothing but useless slaughter of infantry." The British loss had amounted to 50,000 men while their opponents had lost 20,000. The French lost 190,000 against a German loss of 120,000—which was largely caused in ineffective counter-attacks. Both the French and British had gained in experience but they had afforded the enemy still better experience in the way to frustrate such attacks.

The British failure had an important sequel. Even before Loos, Haig's distrust of French had revived and grown, and he had communicated to the highest quarters his opinion of his superior's defects. After Loos he ascribed the failure "solely" to French's "initial mistake in refusing to move up the reserves." In his disgust he wrote privately to Kitchener condemning the Commander-in-Chief, and pulled other strong levers. French's removal followed, and Haig was appointed to succeed him. In thus violating the canons of military propriety, Haig seems to have been moved by a sense of duty combined with a sense of destiny. He felt that he was specially called by God to lead the British Armies to victory. He was as certain of divine help as Hindenburg on the other side, prayed as constantly for it. Their minds worked simply, if their natures were not devoid of complexity.

7. ITALY ENTERS THE WAR

As some compensation for their vain losses the Allied ranks had been swelled by the addition of Italy's forces. In May she had definitely thrown off the artificial ties of the old Triple Alliance and declared war on Austria, her hereditary foe. If her main object was to seize the chance of redeeming Trieste and the Trentino from Austria's rule, there was also a desire to reassert her historic traditions. Militarily, however, her aid could not greatly affect the situation, for her army was unready and the Austrian frontier was a mountainous obstacle of great natural strength. Indeed, on her entry, the Austrians were able to hold her forces without withdrawing more than a few divisions from their offensive front against Russia. Although the Italian commander Cadorna, had a great numerical superiority, he had mountains as well as machine-guns to bar the path of his troops, and all he did was to repeat Joffre's battering-ram tactics with fewer munitions. By December he had lost over a quarter of a million men.

The Italians continued their efforts in 1916, although interrupted in the early summer by a dangerous Austrian stroke in the Asiago region, at the west end of their back-bent line along the Alps; this threatened to burst through into the Venetian plains, but the danger was stalled off. Cadorna then switched his reserves back to the Isonzo, and in August a fresh Italian offensive pushed across the river and captured Gorizia, but attempts to exploit the success eastward broke down. Three more efforts were made in the autumn; if they imposed a wearing strain on the defenders, they caused greater loss to the attackers. During the year the Italians suffered half a million casualties to their opponents' quarter of a million. Still the effort was continued, without adequate munitions or compensating originality of method. By August 1917 they had fought eleven "Battles of the Isonzo"—and were still on the Isonzo.

8. "MESPOT"

Another campaign which developed in 1915, and opened a fresh drain on the British resources, was in Mesopotamia. A diversion of force that had no promise of distraction from the enemy's main concentration, it could only be justified on other than military grounds—to maintain British influence in that part of the world and her oil supply from the fields near the Persian Gulf. Although its origin was sound, its development was another example of "drift," due to the inherent faultiness of Britain's machinery for the conduct of war.

When war with Turkey was imminent a small Indian force was despatched to safeguard the oilfields. To fulfill this mission effectively it was necessary to occupy the Basra vilayet at the head of the Persian Gulf, in order to command the possible lines of approach.

But the British commander, General Nixon, judged it wise to expand his footing, for greater security. Townshend's division was pushed up the Tigris to Amara, gaining a brilliant little victory, and the other division up the Euphrates to Nasiriya. Southern Mesopotamia was a vast alluvial plain, roadless and railless, in which these two great rivers formed the only channels of communication. Thus a hold on Amara and Nasiriya covered the oilfields; but Nixon and the Indian Government, inspired by these successes, decided to push forward to Kut-el-'Amara, a move which was one hundred and eighty miles further into the interior but had a partial military justification in the fact that at Kut the Shatt-el-Hai, issuing from the Tigris, formed a link with the Euphrates by which Turkish reserves could be transferred from one river line to the other.

Townshend was sent forward in August, defeated the Turks near Kut, and his cavalry carried the pursuit to Aziziya, half-way to Baghdad. Enthusiasm spread to the home government, anxious for a moral counterpoise to their other failures, and Nixon thus gained permission for Townshend to press on to Baghdad.

The Turks, now nearly double his strength but shaken in morale, lay in a position near the historic arch of Cresiphon. Townshend's first idea was to manœuvre them out of it, but he was enticed by the idea of winning a famous victory and was confirmed in it by the feeling that the text-book "principle of seeking the bulk of the hostile force in the field" should not be departed from. His attack proved indecisive, but two days later a rumour that the British were moving wide round the flank threw the Turkish commander into a panic, and he issued orders for a hasty retreat, which was made that night in a state of confusion. Townshend, however, had been depressed by his own severe losses in the attack, and also decided to retreat. The Turks, recovering confidence, turned round and followed him—and he continued his retreat, back to Kut. Here he remained after a too optimistic assurance of early relief—several fresh divisions were being sent to Mesopotamia.

Kut was invested by the Turks on December 8th, 1915, and the relieving forces battered in vain against the Turkish lines covering the approach. The conditions were bad, the communications worse, the generalship bungled, and at last on April 29th, 1916, Kut was forced to surrender—after the British Government, on Townshend's inspiration, had made a vain and ill-judged effort to bribe the Turks by an offer of a million pounds, then raised to two, to let the garrison go free. Although censorship kept it from the British public, the Turks took care to broadcast to other peoples the news of this bargaining. The loss in the vain military effort, including Townshend's own, had totalled nearly 40,000 men—a loss nearly double the actual strength of the Turkish force opposing it.

1916

1. THE WESTERN FRONT IN 1916—
VERDUN AND THE SOMME

The lines of the war became simplified in 1916—to what was for the Allies, in strategic aim, virtually a single track. The position of Austria, as well as of Turkey, had been so far secured that its very security now helped the arguments of the "Western school"— that the Allies should concentrate their whole effort on gaining the decision in France. This was now generally accepted as the only feasible course.

When, in June, Joffre suddenly tried to persuade the British Government to enlarge the forces on Salonika, it was Lloyd George himself who supported the General Staff's objections by pointing out that the conditions had essentially changed: that, having lost the chance when Serbia was still intact and Bulgaria uncommitted, the Allies could not at present hope to develop an effective distraction—to Germany's forces—in the Balkans, until they were properly equipped. Against such a barrier as now existed there, mere increase of troops would not avail. To make an impression on the Bulgarian defences sufficient to disturb Germany, the Allied forces would have to be far better equipped than was yet possible. This pricked the bubble project. Joffre's strange and ill-timed change of attitude seems to have been inspired by a desire to divert attention from his own troubles in France, and to propitiate those of his own countrymen who had not forgotten nor forgiven the way he had stultified timely measures in 1915.

There was a heavy bill to pay, not only in lost opportunities, for that obstinate disregard of the wider horizon of war. For the British forces holding Salonika against the Bulgarians, guarding Egypt against the Turks, and vainly endeavouring to relieve Kut, amounted to over half a million men. Such were the extravagant consequences of the refusal to spare the 150,000 needed for the Gallipoli expedition in the spring of 1915. In the light of history there can hardly be a doubt that a force on the scale of Hankey's original estimate would have sufficed to achieve success with a margin to spare—if it had been sent in time.

It was not for want of men that the campaign in France suffered in 1916. Britain's new armies were now approaching full tide, and measures were being taken to keep them up to strength. Unwilling to abandon the principle of voluntary enlistment, the Government had attempted to combine it with a systematic plan, based on a National Register. This scheme, launched in the autumn of 1915 under the auspices of Lord Derby, aimed to reconcile the demands of the Army with the needs of industry, calling up men by groups as they were wanted, and taking single men first. But the response from the bachelors was not adequate and in January 1916, by the Military Service Act, the voluntary "system" was replaced by conscription. The mass army had become a national institution for the duration of the war, and its inauguration finally sealed the tomb of Britain's traditional strategy.

Despite the loss of half a million men, the British strength in France at the beginning of the year had risen to a million. It comprised thirty-eight divisions; by midsummer nineteen more would be added. The French had ninety-five, which with the addition of the Belgians, gave the Allies a total of one hundred and thirty-nine divisions against one hundred and seventeen German divisions of rather smaller man-power. Whereas at the end of 1914 the British had only held twenty-one miles of front out of four hundred and sixty-six, they now held sixty-seven, soon increased to eighty-seven. If this frontage was small in proportion to their strength, giving rise to French complaints that the British required an excessive insurance, it covered a more strategically important area.

In keeping his troops so closely concentrated Haig had an eye also for his offensive aims. But he had to yield his desire for a stroke in Flanders to Joffre's preference for one on the Somme alongside the French. From now onwards there was to be a continual conflict between the French desire that the British should take over more of the front, and Haig's desire to keep his strength for a decisive blow made in his own way.

The close of 1915 saw, however, the first serious attempt to secure unity of action among the Allies as a whole, when in December a conference of the military leaders assembled at Chantilly under Joffre's presidence, Kitchener's hopes of a call to take supreme charge had faded, with his reputation. The conference adopted the principle of a simultaneous general offensive in 1916 on the French, Russian, and Italian fronts. Theoretically, this promised to provide an effective distraction to Germany's concentration in the west. But the actual conditions of Russia's and Italy's situation made it a fading hope. It was recognized that the general offensive could not begin before the summer, because of the need to complete the training of the new British forces and the equipment of the Russian. Joffre planned to strike astride the Somme in July with forty French and twenty-five British divisions. But he was still barren of new ideas that might have helped him in breaking through the trench barrier. More heavy guns, more shells—such was his sole recipe for success.

Even in this he was forestalled—because in February Falkenhayn was at last able to attempt the fulfilment of his own dream of winning the war in the west. More subtle than Joffre, he planned to use his mass of artillery as a mincing-machine. By attacking a point that the French pride would be loth to give up he hoped to draw their reserves into the maw of his guns, and thus bleed France to death. As possible objectives he considered Belfort or Verdun, and chose Verdun—because it offered a salient and so cramped the defender, because it was at present a menace to the main German railway artery (only twelve miles distant), and because of the moral effect if so renowned a place were lost to France. Unfortunately for his design, his executive subordinates had a conventionally military outlook. Misunderstanding its economic basis, and impatient of his inglorious care of lives, they so misapplied his intentions as to spoil the aim in marring the economy.

The keynote of the German tactical plan was a continuous series of limited advances which, by their menace, should draw the French reserves into the mincing-machine of the German artillery. Each of these advances was to be covered by an intense artillery bombardment, brief for surprise and making up for its short duration by the number of batteries and the rapidity of their fire. By this means each objective would be taken and consolidated before the enemy could move up his reserves for counter-attack.

At first the French played into Falkenhayn's hands. Although the French Intelligence branch at General Headquarters gave early warning of the German preparations, the Operations branch were so full of their own offensive schemes that the warning fell on deaf ears. Further, the easy fall of the Belgian and Russian fortresses had led to a commonly held view that fortresses were obsolete, and Joffre, persuading the French Government to declass Verdun as a fortress, had denuded it of guns and troops. The forts were only used as shelters and the trench lines which took their place were inadequate and in poor repair. Yet eight months' bombardment was to leave the forts undamaged!

For some time rumours had percolated to Paris about the state of the Verdun defences, and in December Galliéni, who had been made Minister of War, had asked Joffre for an assurance that they would be improved. Joffre indignantly denied that there was any cause for anxiety, and demanded the names of those who had dared to suggest it: "I cannot be a party to soldiers under my command bringing before the Government, by channels other than the hierarchic channel, complaints or protests about the execution of my orders. . . . It is calculated to disturb profoundly the spirit of discipline in the Army."

On the morning of February 21st the German bombardment began on a front of fifteen miles, and progressively trenches and wire were flattened out or upheaved in a chaos of tumbled earth. Nine hours later a thin chain of German infantry advanced, to feel the strength of the French resistance before the mass of the infantry was launched—a method which economized life. This reconnaisance disclosed that the effect of the bombardment had varied, and the attack was only launched on a narrow sector. Next day it developed more widely and thereafter the defenders' line was crumbled like sand before the erosion of the tide.

Joffre was slow to realize the gravity of the situation, being assured by "Operations" that the attack was merely a feint. On the 24th he retired to bed early as was his habit. But such alarming reports came in that at eleven o'clock Castelnau, greatly daring, insisted that the orderly officer should rap on his door and wake him. Castelnau obtained Joffre's authority to go to Verdun to discover the true situation and take the necessary action. He drove thither in the night.

Joffre meanwhile had telegraphed: "Every commander who . . . gives an order for retreat will be tried by court-martial."

Castelnau swung back the right flank but ordered the line of the forts to be held at all costs and entrusted the defence to Pétain, for whose use a reserve army was assembled. Pétain's first problem was not so much defence as supply—the German heavy guns had closed all avenues into the salient except one light railway and the Bar-le-Duc road. While gangs of territorial troops worked night and day to keep this in repair and widen it, Pétain organized the front into sectors and threw in repeated counter-attacks which, helped by the narrowness of the front, at least slowed down the advance. Falkenhayn sought, somewhat late, to widen the front, and on March 6th the Germans extended the attacks to the west bank of the Meuse. But the defence was now stiffening, the numbers balanced, and the immediate danger to Verdun was checked.

A slight lull followed, and during it the Allies of France made efforts to relieve the pressure upon her. The British took over the Arras front from the French Tenth Army, the Italians made their fifth attack on the Isonzo front, and the Russians hurled untrained masses on the German front at Lake Narocz near Vilna, gallantly sacrificing their troops to help their Allies. These efforts did not prevent Falkenhayn pursuing his attrition offensive at Verdun.

At the end of March the Crown Prince, who was in executive control, confidently declared that the bulk of the French reserves had been exhausted and urged that it was time to complete their destruction by more sweeping methods—"by the employment of men, not merely by the use of machines and munitions." Princely subordinates were hard to control, and Falkenhayn's position was too unstable for him to risk taking a strong line. So he gave way to this plea for a return to old-fashioned methods.

The cost to the Germans mounted, but before long Joffre intervened to restore his own debit balance. He decided that, for prestige, Fort Douaumont must be recovered. He also removed the restraining hand of Pétain—who was promoted to the grade of an Army Group commander—and placed Nivelle in direct charge at Verdun. Repeated attacks caused a fresh drain of French strength. On June 7th Fort Vaux fell and the grey tide crept closer to Verdun. Then on June 20th the Germans introduced a new kind of diphosgene gas-shell: its use paralysed the French artillery support and enabled the Germans to reach the Belleville heights, the last outwork of Verdun. The French command prepared to evacuate the east bank of the Meuse. But the Germans had used their new lever too late.

In Russia a sudden attack by Brusilov's armies had produced a catastrophic Austrian collapse. In order to repair the breach Falkenhayn had to withdraw troops from the Western Front, and thus forgo his hope of continuing to operate the Verdun mincing-machine as well as of delivering a counter-stroke against the forthcoming British offensive. On June 24th the prepara-

tory bombardment opened on the Somme; that day
Falkenhayn stopped the flow of ammunition to Verdun. On July 1st the offensive itself began. No fresh
German divisions were sent to Verdun. The machine
slowed down and stopped. It had devoured some
315,000 Frenchmen compared with a German loss of
281,000. If this was the only prolonged offensive on
the Western Front where the attackers' cost was less
than the defenders', the margin was hardly large
enough to make the attrition method strategically
economic.

Nevertheless it had so far drawn in the French reserves as to reduce seriously their share in the Somme
plan. Their intended front of attack shrank from
twenty-five miles to eight, and their force from forty
divisions to sixteen, of which only five took part in the
original attack. From this time forward the British
took over, in effort if not in front, the main burden
of the campaign in France. Because of this fact alone
July 1st, 1916, is a landmark in the history of the war.
It is also an obelisk—marking the graveyard of "Kitchener's Army," that great band of citizen volunteers
who, answering the call in 1914, had formed the first
national army of Britain.

2. THE SOMME OFFENSIVE

Haig entrusted his main attack on the Somme to
Rawlinson's Fourth Army: eleven divisions were
to lead the assault, on a fourteen-mile front, with five
more close up in support. This gave the British a

superiority of over six to one against the German troops holding that sector, which could be increased if the reserves—four infantry and three cavalry divisions—were thrown in early. Allenby's army would help by a subsidiary attack near Gonnecourt. The artillery concentration totalled over 1500 guns—a gun to every twenty yards of front, which was a record at that time. But for pulverizing the defences of what was the strongest sector of the Western Front, heavy artillery was needed: and its proportion was not so impressive. Whereas the French for their neighbouring attack had over nine hundred heavy guns, the British had barely half this number for a wider front. But they suffered greater handicaps than that—handicaps that, to avoid any suspicion of exaggeration, can best be told in the mild accents of the Official History.

The problem which confronted Haig was, fundamentally, that of "storming a fortress. . . . It must be confessed that the problem was not appreciated at G.H.Q." The cause, in part, lay in the pre-war current of military thought. "It must be admitted that the problems of semi-siege warfare and the large concentration of guns necessary for the attack of great field defences had never been studied in peace-time by the General Staff. Under the influence of General H. H. Wilson (the late Sir Henry Wilson) it had been content to follow French ideas as to the nature of the next war, and ignored and almost resented hearing of the information obtained by its Intelligence Branch as to the preparations being made and methods practised as manœuvres by the Germans." A more immediate cause lay in the failure of the Higher Command to grasp the main lesson of two years' hard experience —a lesson that was well appreciated by front-line soldiers: "The failures of the past were put down to reasons other than the stout use of the machine-gun by the enemy and his scientifically-planned defences." Such expert "reasoning" is certainly one of the most remarkable examples in all history, of the wood being missed for the trees.

Thus was produced, once again, an atmosphere of false confidence. It encouraged Haig to gamble on a "break-through." But Rawlinson's more reasonable doubts led to the plan becoming a compromise, suited neither to a swift penetration nor to a siege-attack. He desired a long bombardment and a short advance. He was eventually allowed the first, but was overborne by Haig on the second, being instructed that on his left he should take both the German first and second positions at a single bite—although Haig was warned even by his own Artillery Adviser that he was "stretching" his available gun-power too far. "Rawlinson assured the Commander-in-Chief that he would loyally carry out 'these instructions.' But privately he was convinced that they were based on false premises, and on too great optimism. . . ." The outcome was to show the danger of this kind of loyalty.

"Increasing optimism" was shown by Haig as the day of battle drew nearer, although the resources of the French, and consequently their prospective contribution, were steadily shrinking owing to the drain of Verdun. It was shown even in the additional instructions he issued. The cavalry was to ride through to Bapaume on the first morning, into open country. The main army would reach this in its second bound and would then wheel north to roll up the German front as far as Arras.

More curious than Haig's optimism was the way Rawlinson joined him in assuring their subordinates repeatedly that the bombardment would swamp all resistance and that "the infantry would only have to walk over and take possession." Such bland assurance was more than natural loyalty demanded. Haig, indeed, had suggested that, following the German method at Verdun, the effect of the bombardment might be tested by sending ahead an advance chain of patrols before the thick waves of infantry were launched. This precaution was "rejected by his army commanders." In the early discussions Haig had also said that the "corps were not to attack until their commanders were satisfied that the enemy's defences had been sufficiently destroyed; but this condition seems to have been dropped as time passed."

The plan definitely abandoned the essential element of surprise. Even if the prolonged bombardment had not given the enemy ample warning the preparations were unconcealed. Yet they seem to have had the effect of an unintentional double bluff. For they were so blatant as to suggest a deception. And Falkenhayn was convinced that the attack on the Somme was only a preliminary to the real blow further north— for which Haig had made less obvious preparations. In consequence, Falkenhayn withheld reinforcements

—and thus restored a measure of opportunity to his opponent.

The use of this opportunity still depended on the ability of the British to overwhelm the sparse defenders. Unfortunately Rawlinson, while questioning whether he had sufficient heavy artillery for his frontage, had spread it evenly over the front—"without regard to the strength and importance of any particular part." The result was that "their fire was necessarily so dispersed that many strong points and machine-gun posts were never touched."

Thus the remaining chances of success depended on whether the infantry could reach the enemy trenches before the defenders could open fire. There were two ways in which this might have been achieved: by crossing either before the enemy could see to fire or before they were ready to fire. Without fog, natural or artificial, the only chance of the first lay in an assault during the darkness or in the dim light before dawn. We learn that "a few commanders . . . desired that at least the assault should be made at the first streak of light, before the enemy machine-gunners could see their prey." We are told that "Rawlinson himself accepted" the suggestion "and pressed his French neighbours to agree." But they had double his quantity of heavy guns and wanted good observation for them. So he agreed to the later hour, apparently with little misgiving.

The question that remained was whether the British infantry could cross no-man's land before the barrage lifted. It was a race with death run by nearly

sixty thousand men in the first heat. They were hope-
lessly handicapped. The whole mass, made up of close-
ly-packed waves of men, was to be launched together,
without discovering whether the bombardment had
really paralysed the resistance. Under the Fourth
Army's instructions, those waves were to advance at
"a steady pace," symmetrically aligned, like rows of
nine-pins ready to be knocked over. "The necessity
of crossing no-man's land at a good pace, so as to reach
the parapet before the enemy could reach it, was not
mentioned." Yet to do so would have been physically
impossible, for the heaviest handicap of all was that
"the infantryman was so heavily laden that he could
not move faster than a walk." Each man carried about
66 lb., over half his own body weight, "which made
it difficult to get out of a trench, impossible to move
much quicker than a slow walk, or to rise and lie
down quickly."

The race was lost before it started, and the battle
soon after. The barrage went on, the infantry could
not go on, the barrage could not be brought back, and
infantry reinforcements were pushed in just where no
infantry could push on. Moreover, "the tactical plan
of the battle was too rigid," and too uniform in its
distribution of force. No latitude was allowed for elasticity or initiative in exploiting local advantages, or
in adjusting the artillery arrangements.

In the south, near the Somme, the French made
good progress, helped by a cloaking river-mist. So did
the XIIIth Corps on their left. It could have gone on,
for opportunity yawned wide, but the French pro-

posal to continue the advance did not find favour with the British higher command. Further north, the XVth Corps had a harder task—to pinch out Fricourt—but attained a partial success at heavy cost. And there success ended. Sixty thousand men had paid forfeit for the plan that failed—the heaviest day's loss that a British army ever suffered. That result, and its causes, cast a strange reflection on the words which Haig had written on the eve of the attack: "I feel that every step in my plan has been taken with the Divine help." This tragic day had at least furnished proof of the moral quality of these citizen-soldiers of Britain. They had borne a percentage of loss such as no army of the past had ever been deemed capable of withstanding, unbroken.

Behind the front the higher commanders had been rendering reports rosier than the facts warranted, and also, apparently, than the commanders themselves believed. "Captures of prisoners, but not the heavy casualties, were regularly reported." Ignorance in such conditions was natural, but deception less excusable.

As for the opportunity of developing such success as had been obtained in the south, this went begging. "No orders or instructions were issued during the day by Fourth Army Headquarters' save on a few minor details. At 10 p.m. Rawlinson merely ordered his corps to "continue the attack" uniformly. "No suggestion was made to utilize the successes gained by some to assist in improving the situation of those which had failed."

A fresh opportunity offered on July 14th, but was

not.taken. It was created by Rawlinson's initiative, in face of the doubts expressed by Haig and the French, in attempting to storm the Germans' second position, on the right, by a night approach across an exposed area, followed by an assault in the first faint gleam of dawn: the assault preceded by a hurricane bombardment of only a few minutes' duration. This was a gamble in accord with the true nature of war for it took due account of the value of surprise. And the novelty proved brilliantly successful. But the tardy attempt to exploit it proved that the second half of the problem was not yet understood.

After this fresh disappointment Haig played for smaller stakes, carrying out a series of local attacks until he was ready for a further large effort. The process was called "attrition" although the method was essentially different from, and more expensive than, Falkenhayn's design. But zealous propaganda for this new titular deity of war spread faith in its effects. It covered up the costly failure of another big attack on July 23rd. It would also cover up, until long after the war, the fact that Haig's original aim had been, and became again, a break-through.

On August 30th Rawlinson noted in his diary: "The Chief is anxious to have a gamble with all the available troops about September 15th, with the object of breaking down German resistance and getting through to Bapaume." He added, somewhat illogically: "We shall have no reserves in hand, save tired troops, but success at this time . . . might bring the Boches to terms." Despite his professed faith in attrition, Haig was now reduced to gambling on a break-through. To increase its chances he utilized a new weapon—the "tank." This was the camouflage name given to the armoured fighting vehicles which had been invented as an antidote to the defensive combination of machine-guns and barbed-wire. Colonel Swinton had been the father and Churchill the mother of the idea, although numerous god-parents and grandparents deserve a share of the credit—for it suffered prolonged obstruction before it came to maturity in the machine of which Mr. Tritton and Lieutenant Wilson were the designers. Unfortunately, the desire for anything that might redeem the fading prospects of the Somme now led to its premature use. Swinton had insisted on the importance of waiting until the tank was ready, and in sufficient numbers to gain the full effect of its surprise appearance. Haig had expressed his agreement with this principle which he now forsook.

A handful of the new machines helped, despite their mechanical defects, towards the partial success obtained on September 15th, and again on the 25th.

This was not sufficient, however, to check instinctive doubts of such an unfamiliar weapon. An adverse report from G.H.Q. caused Robertson to cancel the order for a thousand that had recently been given. That counter-order, however, went to a temporary soldier who, emboldened by his established civil position, went straight to the War Minister—to find that the cancellation had been made behind his back. The building order was reinstated. Before long the tempo-

rary soldier would be shifted from his post, and so
would Swinton—but the tank went on: to become,
by German verdict, the most dangerous and decisive
of the weapons employed against them.

The Somme offensive foundered in the mud when
November came, although its dismal finale was partially redeemed by the bright flash of a stroke delivered on November 13th by Gough's recently formed
army on the still untouched flank of the main offensive. The four months' struggle had certainly imposed
a severe strain on the German resistance, as well as on
the attackers. Both armies had lost vast quantities of
men who in quality would never be replaced. The
British losses amounted to some 420,000. The French,
who had played an increasing part in the later stages,
had raised their war-casualty bill by 194,000. Against
this Allied total of over 600,000 the Germans had suffered something over 440,000. This proportion, like
the strain they suffered, had been much increased by
the action of General von Bülow who had issued an
order, soldierly but not sane, that every yard of lost
trench must be retaken by counter-attack. This had
much helped the British artillery to improve its practice at the expense of the German infantry.

3. THE RUSSIAN AND BALKAN
FRONTS IN 1916

After 1915 the Entente could no longer indulge in
dreams of the Russian steam-roller rolling on to
Berlin. The most that could be expected of Russia

was that she might pin down sufficient German forces to enable the French and British to gain a superiority in the west. In the spring she was holding forty-six German and forty Austrian divisions on her front, and was preparing for her promised offensive in July. But these plans were once more upset by the enemy's initiative in another theatre.

For 1916, the Austrian command had urged the German to join it in an attempt to follow their combined success against Serbia by wiping Italy off the board. Conrad pointed out that the Venetian theatre of war lent itself to a decisive thrust south from the Trentino against the rear of the Italian armies. A year later, events would tend to support his prediction, and the dramatic effect of a comparatively light thrust would suggest that another of the war's great opportunities had been missed—this time by the Central Powers. For Falkenhayn doubted Conrad's plan, preferring to pursue his own at Verdun. So he withheld the divisions Conrad needed, while Conrad withheld the howitzers Falkenhayn needed for Verdun.

Unwilling to be baulked, Conrad weakened his front against Russia by drawing off some of his best divisions, yet without securing the measure of force needed for his Italian plan. He was helped at the outset by Cadorna's disregard of warnings. The Italian Commander-in-Chief refused to believe the many reports he received that the Austrians were actually concentrating in the Trentino. They struck on May 15th, and they came not far short of breaking through into the plains. The crisis was only averted by the hasty switching of the bulk of the Italian reserves from the Isonzo. When the struggle ended in July the Italians, owing to their initial forfeit of prisoners and subsequent loss in counter-attacking, had lost 150,000 men (and 300 guns) to the Austrians' 80,000.

Italy's emergency had produced an appeal for such indirect aid as Russia could offer. It came at an awkward moment, for the Russians had wasted so much force in their March offensive on behalf of the French that the prospects of their bigger effort were impaired. In the plan of this summer offensive Brusilov's southern group of armies in Galicia was intended merely to distract the enemy's attention from a main blow, planned for delivery in the north.

The Italian appeal hastened Brusilov's action. His was an unconventional plan, which dismayed his own superiors. Although he had bare equality of force he distributed it widely instead of concentrating narrowly in proportion to his means. He made preparations at more than a score of different places, so that deserters should not give away his aim. The absence of warning and of preliminary concentration lulled the Austrians into a false security: and when Brusilov's troops suddenly advanced on June 4th, the hostile front collapsed. In three weeks he had taken a quarter of a million prisoners.

But the reserves were massed in the north and the army group commanders there were dilatory in striking. When the Supreme Command tried to divert the reserves to back up Brusilov, the poor rail communications delayed their arrival. German reinforcements helped to fill the gap, and when the Russians were able to renew their effort they paid the usual penalty for such belated attacks. In the end the loss outweighed the gain, mounting to a million casualties, and thus hastening the revolt against martial massacre which culminated in the Revolution.

Nevertheless, the indirect effects abroad had been large. This threat had compelled Falkenhayn to withdraw seven divisions from the west, to the detriment of his plans there. His bitterness led him to lay the blame on Conrad and procure his removal. His own fall soon followed, as a further indirect consequence. For the Russians' dramatic achievement emboldened Roumania to take her delayed decision to make common cause with the Entente, profiting by Austria's weakness. She entered the war on August 27th. She became another sacrifice to the illusion of mass.

4. THE CONQUEST OF ROUMANIA

During the two years since the outbreak of the war Roumania had doubled the numbers of her army, but her large and clumsy divisions were pitiably weak in modern armament and equipment. Her handicaps were increased by geography, for her frontier was of immense length, and the most important part of her territory was sandwiched between Austrian Transylvania and Bulgaria, whose frontier lay within thirty miles of her capital.

Prompted by her own ambitions and Russian advice, Roumania's main armies advanced westward over the Carpathians into Transylvania. If they could have moved quicker, they might have placed Austria in grave peril, for she had only a few weak divisions to meet them. But their own caution and delays, increased by the enemy's demolition of the bridges, kept them at a distance while the Austro-German command was collecting a picked force for a counter-offensive, and providing a Bulgar force with technical equipment as well as an expert staff. On September 5th, while the Roumanian columns were creeping westward, the Bulgarian force under Mackensen stormed the Roumanians' bridgehead south of the Danube; then, with his own flank secure Mackensen turned eastward and invaded the Dobruja, Roumania's "backyard" on the Black Sea. This menace drew the Roumanians' reserves in a long distance chase after him, thus uncovering their southern frontier and weakening their western offensive.

The opportunity was seized by Falkenhayn who, on his replacement in the Supreme Command by the partnership of Hindenburg and Ludendorff, had been given command of the counter-offensive in Transylvania. Striking at the paralysed Roumanian masses, he threw them back on the Carpathians. But he missed his aim of cutting them off, and was blocked at the mountain passes. This failure nearly wrecked the whole German plan. But in mid-November, just before the winter snows sealed the passes, a last minute effort succeeded in breaking through. Then, while Falkenhayn pursued his invasion eastwards through the plains towards Bucharest, Mackensen initiated the next move in the combined plan. Switching his forces back from the Dobruja, on November 23rd, he forced the crossings of the Danube at Sistovo, south-west of Bucharest. Thence he converged against the forces opposing Falkenhayn; under the double pressure these gave way, and on December 6th the Roumanian capital fell into the invader's hands. Following up their advantage they swept the defeated armies back to the Sereth, thus gaining possession of the greater part of Roumania with its wheat and oil.

This fresh success against one of the Allies' junior partners loaded the strategy of the senior partners with a still heavier burden. By clearing another piece off the board, it enabled the Germans to concentrate more easily to resist the Franco-British concentration in the west. And by securing Roumania's material resources it strengthened the foundations upon which the Germans' power of resistance rested. Thus, ironically, the Western Powers' determination in sacrificing everything else to the pursuit of a decisive victory in the west augmented year by year the strength of the opposition they had still to overcome.

5. THE MIDDLE EAST

The "Western" doctrine, which had departed so far from Britain's tradition, found its very embodiment in Sir William Robertson, the cavalry sergeant-major who had risen by some twenty years of sheer application to be Chief of the Imperial General Staff, and the director of the British Empire's strategy in the greatest of her tests. His desire to concentrate exclusively in the west was nevertheless frustrated— less by political opposition than by the inherent resistance of strategic and imperial conditions. A considerable part of the British forces were tied to the Middle East by the need, so long as Turkey was hostile, of protecting British interests there. Robertson's efforts to restrict these forces proved more effective in fettering their action than in helping his own purpose. The defence of Egypt and of the Persian Gulf changed gradually into an offensive in both theatres as the defects and dangers of passive defence became clearer. But it was an uneconomic form of offensive.

Lloyd George and others may have overrated the damage that the defeat of Turkey would have caused to Germany: materially she was not a "prop" in the sense that Austria was, although morally she may have become one. But Robertson certainly underrated the help to his own plans which might have come through the release of British forces in the Middle East, a release that could only come by the overthrow of Turkey. By operating with large forces against her extremities the effect was inevitably slow without the expense being kept low. By degrees these campaigns in Palestine and Mesopotamia became a process in which two British armies, wriggling across the desert like giant pythons, gradually swallowed Turkey from the feet up—each taking a leg.

After the fall of Kut, Robertson wisely stopped all operations in Mesopotamia until the forces there were reorganized and their communications improved. In

August General Maude was sent out to take command. He was Robertson's choice and well advised of Robertson's policy, but like most commanders he was susceptible to his immediate horizon, and by subtle if unconscious steps he succeeded in changing that defensive policy into a fresh one of advance upon Baghdad.

With forces restored and enlarged, Maude began in December a methodical series of small attacks to loosen the Turks' position on the west bank of the Tigris. By February, 1917, he was well placed for an attempt to cut off the retreat of their main forces on the east bank. On the 23rd, his left wing forced the passage in their rear, but was then checked by a few well-sited machine-guns; and his right wing was more successful in hastening the enemy's retreat than in holding them. Some naval gunboats, daringly pushing up the river, threw the retreating forces into confusion; but the cavalry, faint in pursuit, failed to profit by their opportunity. Nevertheless, if Maude had failed in his aim of destroying the enemy's force, his strategic success gained him permission to press on to Baghdad. And although the Turks had rallied sufficiently to impose a fresh check, they could not long resist such overwhelming force as he possessed. On March 10th they abandoned the City of the Caliphs, and next afternoon Maude's entry inscribed a British name on the long roll of its conquerors.

Although this achievement bore testimony to improved organization, and was distinguished by careful planning, its value as a military feat was somewhat discounted by the fact that Maude had a superiority of over six to one in fighting strength and far more in total strength, besides greatly superior equipment. This explains why the Turks, better aware of the discrepancy than the British public, cherished a singular respect for Townshend as the only British general who had ever beaten them with inferior strength. If the capture of Baghdad was hailed by the public with applause in excess of its merits, this was due to the sense of relief after two years of depressing failure to attain tangible success elsewhere: as a stimulant its value was not so far short of its cost.

While a quarter of a million men were being fed in Mesopotamia to sustain the advance to Baghdad, an equal number was being maintained in Egypt as an insurance against the menace of a few thousand Turks in Sinai—who became magnified by the mirage of the desert—and that of the Senussi in the Western Desert. Incited by the Turks, the Senussi took the offensive in November, 1915, and caused the British to evacuate several of their posts along the Mediterranean coast; although defeated in February they were not finally quelled until a year later, when a force of armoured cars penetrated to their remote focal point in the Sinai oasis. The possibility of a Turkish invasion of Egypt from the east was even more disturbing to the British command in Egypt, which had been taken over by Sir Archibald Murray. In February, 1916 he estimated that the Turks might bring a quarter of a million men against him, and was not inclined to listen to officers with local knowledge who asked how such a mass could be brought across the desert. In April a force of 3500 Turks under Kress von Kressenstein, a daring and resourceful Bavarian colonel, advanced across the desert and tweaked Murray's nose by surprising and overwhelming several of the posts that covered the approach to the Suez Canal. In July he repeated the attempt, with 16,000 men, but this time lingered too long and suffered a narrow escape from being cut off at Romani; here he was severely mauled, but succeeded in giving his pursuers a sharp rap.

Murray now began to ponder the idea of advancing to the Palestine border, encouraged by news of a distant development which promised to distract the overestimated forces of the enemy. This was the revolt of the Sherif of Mecca, who in June had thrown off the Turkish yoke in the Hejaz. By the autumn this rising on the Red Sea coast was in danger of collapse, and the recapture of Mecca was threatened by a reinforced Turkish expedition. It looked as if the British would again be compelled to despatch forces to the relief of a small Ally—and, probably, again too late. But this time both risks were averted by the diversion of one man, a young archæologist turned temporary soldier, who was known as T. E. Lawrence. He had been an irritation to the orthodox members of Murray's staff, but in Arabia he became a far worse irritation to the Turks. Brilliantly unconventional, deeply read in the history and theory of warfare, and gifted with a magnetic personality, he succeeded in combining the spasmodic and irregular efforts of the Arabs so that the flame of revolt was spread eventually through a thousand miles of the desert, consuming the resources of the Turks as they strove to protect their railway lifeline from the raids he guided or inspired.

In December, when a railway and a pipe-line had at last been laid across the desert, the British massively advanced and occupied El Arish, following this move by the capture of the fortified posts at Magdhaba and Rafah, to which the Turks had withdrawn. In each of these fights the British commander had actually ordered a withdrawal only to find that his men had succeeded. This threw a significant light on what was to follow. For on March 26th the British attacked Gaza, the gateway to Palestine. With a superiority of nine to one they had no difficulty in surrounding the town, whose garrison was about to surrender when they found that the British had withdrawn, called off by their commanders. The damage was increased because Murray reported the affair to the Government in terms of a victory, and was thus spurred to attempt in April a fresh attack which proved a costlier failure against defences now strengthened. The moral effect was serious, and the material loss was not slight—nearly 10,000 British to 3500 Turks, in the two battles. To retrieve the effect the British forces were strongly reinforced, and Murray was replaced by a new commander, Sir Edmund Allenby.

The prospects of the campaign were improved by an unassisted stroke on the part of Lawrence and a few of the Arab chiefs; after raising a few hundred men in the Syrian desert, they descended upon and

captured Aqaba, a port on the northern arm of the
Red Sea. In this coup, they killed and captured 1200
Turks at a cost of two killed in their own force. The
strategic effect was to remove all danger to the British
communications in Sinai and to open the way for the
Arabs to become a lever on the flank of the Turkish
forces who were blocking the British. Already, more
Turks were occupied in guarding the long line of the
Hejaz railway and the territory south of it against a
few handfuls of British-directed Arabs that were facing the mass of the British Army in Palestine. In this
war of the desert there was a curious likeness to the
sea-warfare practised by the Elizabethan sea-captains
and the German U-boat commanders. Camel-raiding
parties in the one element played the same game as
submarines in the other, the main difference being
that the former were careful to avoid killing non-
combatants.

6. THE WAR ON THE SEAS, 1915-1916

Germany's first submarine campaign—associated
by allied opinion with the name of Admiral von
Tirpitz, the exponent of ruthlessness—had borne
meagre results and done disproportionate moral damage to the German cause. A series of notes exchanged
between the American and the German Governments
culminated in April, 1916 in a virtual ultimatum
from President Wilson, and Germany abandoned her
unrestricted campaign. The deprivation of this weapon spurred the German Navy to its first, and last, at-

tempt to carry out its initial plan. On May 30th, 1916, the British Grand Fleet left its bases under Admiral Jellicoe with reason to expect a possible encounter. On May 31st, early in the morning, the German High Sea Fleet also put to sea, in the hope of destroying some isolated portion of the British fleet, using its battle-cruiser force as a bait.

From the outbreak of the war British naval strategy was governed, rightly, by the fact that maintenance of sea supremacy was even more vital than defeat of the German fleet. That sea supremacy had come into force, instantaneously, and upon it was based the whole war effort of Britain, and her Allies, Churchill has epitomized the issue in a graphic phrase: "Jellicoe was the only man on either side who could lose the war in an afternoon." Hence the aim and desire to defeat the German fleet was always subsidiary. If it could be achieved it might do much to hasten the victory of the Allies. But if, in trying to defeat the German fleet, the British lost so heavily as to lose its strategic superiority national defeat would be certain.

The aim of German naval strategy since August, 1914 had been to avoid the risk of a decisive action until the British fleet was so weakened that the prospect of success veered from gloomy to fair. Mines and torpedoes were the means on which the Germans relied to achieve this preliminary weakening. And it was the fear of such under-water weapons, the possibility that by trap or chance they might dramatically alter the balance of strength, which infused an extra degree of prudence into the British strategy of precaution.

The Battle of Jutland. Early in the afternoon of May 31st, Beatty, with his battle-cruisers and a squadron of battleships, after a sweep to the south was turning north to rejoin Jellicoe, when he sighted the German battle-cruisers, five in number. In the initial engagement two of Beatty's six battle-cruisers were hit in vital parts, and when thus weakened he came upon the main German fleet under Admiral von Scheer. He turned north to lure them into reach of Jellicoe, fifty miles distant, who raced to support him.

Owing to errors in reckoning their respective positions, Jellicoe's deployment was complicated. Nevertheless it had a promise of placing him across the head of the enemy's line—the historic manœuvre of "crossing the T"—when Scheer (at 6-30 p.m.) evaded the danger by a sudden turn-about on the part of each ship, almost simultaneously, under cover of a torpedo attack and a smoke screen. Before he was swallowed in the mist he had destroyed another British battle-cruiser. But he had been forced to retire westwards— away from his own harbours. Jellicoe cautiously came round in a curve to follow him.

Half an hour later the German fleet suddenly re-emerged from the mist—opposite the British centre, owing to a miscalculation. Scheer hastily performed another somersault turn, covering it not only by a destroyer attack but also by launching his battle-cruisers in a "death-ride." His escape was helped by Jellicoe's coincident turn-away to avoid the torpedo menace: if this precaution was essential it was certainly a confession of the ease with which the action of the greatest of naval instruments could be thwarted and even paralysed by an infinitely smaller and cheaper one. Only one of the German destroyers was sunk, but the battle-cruisers suffered badly.

Jellicoe was still across his enemy's line of retreat, but had again lost touch with him in the gathering darkness. This cloak of obscurity suggested to some British sailors the possibility and opportunity of launching their own superior torpedo force against the hostile battle-fleet: even if such an attack had done no serious material damage it would have hindered and upset the enemy's movements towards regaining his base. But Jellicoe had laid down the rule that the destroyer flotillas were to be used defensively until the enemy was beaten by gunfire. On taking up his dispositions for the night, he continued to confine his destroyers to a defensive role, massing them five miles astern, for their own security and his, as a pendent tail.

There were three likely routes that the enemy might take during the night and Jellicoe chose a "beat" which reconciled as far as possible the difficulties of covering all. By the course he took the best chance for the enemy was to slip behind him and take the Horn Reefs passage. Yet Jellicoe was curiously insensitive to signs that the enemy was taking this direction. From 10-20 p. m. onwards the British tail was repeatedly in action with the enemy, who eventually broke through at 11-30 p. m. although harassed by the British destroyers for more than an hour longer. From the light craft, hotly engaged, only one report of these encounters came to Jellicoe before midnight; the rearmost British battleships made no report although they were close enough to note construction details of the German battleships. The firing was heard and the flashes seen from Jellicoe's flagship. Yet he made only one enquiry, at 10-46 p. m. as to the source of the firing—and the wording of his signal suggests a preconceived idea that it was merely a hostile destroyer attack. Soon after 11 p. m. he received from the Admiralty, which had been intercepting the German wireless messages, a report which stated that the German fleet was making for home, and gave its dispositions, course, and speed. But he paid no attention to this, perhaps because an earlier message had given, through a slip, an obviously incorrect location.

If Jellicoe had some cause to complain of the sparse information he received from his subordinates, his lack of suspicion is the measure of his responsibility, as it was the salvation of Scheer. The Grand Fleet continued on its southward course as inflexibly as a sentry of ceremonial palace guard, while the German was steaming east into safety. At dawn when the Grand Fleet turned about, it found an empty sea.

A decisive victory might have helped to shorten the slow and costly process of exhaustive slaughter on land. But this one naval battle of the World War was, as a battle, negligible. To trace to it the ultimate surrender of the German fleet two and a half years later is to confuse mere sequence with causation. If the close of the battle saw the German fleet back in harbour while the Grand Fleet rode the sea, the Germans were able to console themselves with the fact that while es-

caping a knock-out they had scored more points than a
foe of much superior strength and immense prestige.
Their new and untried navy had shown itself not inferior in technical efficiency to one which possessed a
matchless tradition. And in the eyes of the world,
which appreciates tangible more easily than intang-
ible effects, the comparison of points scored made
more impression, to the detriment of British naval
prestige, than the fact that the Grand Fleet still
reigned in "command" of the surface of the sea.

Moreover, that command was, like constitutional
sovereignty, subject to important limitations. Instead
of being able, as in the past, to lie continuously so
close to the enemy's ports that his ships could not put
to sea, the investing fleet was now faced by the coun-
ter-threat of the torpedo and the mine to stay at a safe
distance. It lay normally in protected harbours of its
own where it afforded distant cover to the smaller
craft controlling the trade-routes, and whence it might
hope to intercept any sortie of the enemy's battle-fleet
before this could do serious damage. Although Britain's geographical position lying like a giant breakwater across the sea-approaches to Germany, helped
her to exercise this distant control, it was by no means
impermeable. In April the Chief of the Naval Staff
had confessed that the Germans practically commanded the North Sea south of the Tyne and were repeatedly making sweeps which the British could not coun-
ter. In the words of the Official History: "The Grand
Fleet could only put to sea with an escort of nearly
one hundred destroyers, no capital ship could leave its

base without an escort of small craft, and the German U-boats had hampered our squadrons to an extent which the most experienced and far-sighted naval officer had never foreseen."

Less than three months after Jutland the German Fleet came out again, and came within close reach of the English coast without being brought to battle. The Grand Fleet hastened south from Scapa to meet it but on running into a submarine ambush, and losing one of the advanced line of cruisers, Jellicoe turned and steamed north for two hours, forfeiting the opportunity. Subsequently the Grand Fleet was debarred by its own orders from venturing into the southern half of the North Sea. In October 1916 the German fleet made another extensive sally which the Grand Fleet made no attempt to intercept. That autumn, when the danger of a German invasion of Denmark was discussed, examination of the problem by the Admiralty led to the conclusion that "for naval reasons it would be almost impossible to support the Danes at all." The chief of the reasons given was that, in face of submarine attack, the British fleet could not take the risk of protecting the transport of troops and their line of communication.

The impression which Jutland left on the German naval leaders had even more far-reaching effects. On July 4th Scheer had reported to the Kaiser that: "The disadvantages of our geographical situation—and the enemy's vast material superiority—cannot be coped with to such a degree as to make us masters of the blockade inflicted on us . . . A victorious end to the

war at not too distant a date can only be looked for by
the crushing of English economic life through U-boat
action against English commerce." "As English economic life depended on sea trade, the only means of
getting at it was to overcome the fleet, or get past it.
The former meant the destruction of the fleet, which,
in view of our relative strength was not possible. . . .
The U-boats, however, could get past the fleet."

The submarine campaign was therefore actively
continued, with increasing effect despite increasing
counter-measures. During a single week of September
over thirty British and neutral merchant ships were
sunk in the channel by two or three submarines, who
themselves suffered no loss, although the area was
watched by nearly six hundred destroyers and patrol
craft. The fact that so few submarines could inflict
such disproportionate injury was a strong argument
for using more on this work. Germany, however, had
not got sufficient both to wage this indirect attack and
to protect the sorties of her battle-fleet. So the fleet
henceforth had to stay in harbour. The British were
also placed in a dilemma: if they were to provide sufficient destroyers to escort the Grand Fleet they would
limit their chances of resisting the attack on their supplies. "A deadlock had thus been reached, and it
seemed that for the future the two great battle-fleets
could but lie inactive, watching one another across a
kind of 'no-man's sea,' where attack and defence were
concerned only with transport and commerce."

The German naval leaders now urged that an unrestricted campaign against commerce should be re-

sumed. They were encouraged by the strong American protests against the British blockade's interference with neutral trade, and by the feeling that the influence of British naval prestige had been shaken by Jutland. The German statesmen opposed this naval argument, and several of them were convinced that it was now to Germany's interest to seize a favourable moment for negotiating peace on a fairly conciliatory basis. But military and naval propaganda was vigorously employed to counteract their influence, while the censorship was used to prevent the public hearing any critical doubts.

When Hindenburg and Ludendorff took over the supreme command a conference was assembled at Pless early in September. Here Admiral Holtzendorff, the Chief of the Naval Staff, took the opportunity to press his case for unrestricted submarine warfare—in which all ships would be sunk without warning, thus avoiding the risk that the attacker ran under the rule of "visit and search." The Foreign Minister, Jagow, replied: "Germany will be treated like a mad dog against which everybody combines." Helfferich emphasizing the dangers of bringing America in, declared: "I can see in the employment of the U-boat weapon nothing but catastrophe." Holtzendorff replied: "I am convinced—I cannot adduce any proof—that a fortnight's unrestricted U-boat war will have this effect, that the neutrals will keep aloof from England." Jagow was not impressed by this confident prediction. He argued that: "The difference between our methods and England's is, above all, to be found in the fact that we should be destroying ships and human life in order to exert pressure, whereas by the English method the neutrals are only restricted in the free exercise of their activity."

The next week an envoy of the Naval Staff visited Ludendorff, to win over his support, and came away persuaded that "General Ludendorff believes in a successful issue to submarine war." The Chancellor, Bethmann Hollweg, realizing that his powers of resistance were declining, obtained the Kaiser's permission to make a peace-move in America. But the military and naval leaders were of one mind in their determination to obstruct such a diplomatic step, and when Holtzendorff was curtly told by the Kaiser that the idea of resuming the unrestricted submarine campaign must be postponed, he succeeded in gaining the General Staff to join him in a campaign against the Chancellor's authority. It is doubtful whether Hindenburg and Ludendorff shared his faith in the submarine campaign: it is certain that they were determined to be the deciding authority.

The conditions of peace now settled upon by Germany and Austria were that: Belgium must be evacuated but was, in return, to give certain undefined securities to Germany—the generals were insisting on control of the railways as well as a heavy indemnity. France would be given back her invaded provinces but was to pay an indemnity and also give up the Briey Basin. The greater part of Serbia was to be given to Bulgaria and the remainder tied economically to Austria. Russia was to cede all provinces occupied by

the German armies which were either to be annexed
or set up as independent states bound closely to Germany. The captured German colonies were to be returned with the exception of the Japanese acquisi-
tions. In compensation for these Belgium was to cede
Germany the Congo. Far as these terms went beyond
the possibility of acceptance, the military leaders only
passed them with private reservations—for example
that "Belgium must remain as a strategical area for
protection of the most important German industrial
district and as Hinterland for our position on the
Flanders coast, which is indispensable to our maritime importance." The Kaiser was of the same opinion. "The coast of Flanders must become ours."

A few days after the discreetly vague German Peace
Note had been despatched, and almost simultaneously
with President Wilson's offer to mediate, Hindenburg
and Ludendorff decided to force the Chancellor's
hand and frustrate his peace-aim by launching the
submarine campaign forthwith. They had come to
doubt whether the war could be won on land before
the economic front collapsed. The food shortage seems
to have been the main ground of their conclusion, although the immediate impulse, according to Ludendorff's statement later, was the unexpected success of
the French attack at Verdun on December 15th. This
and a previous attack on October 24th retook in a
couple of bites most of the ground which had been
captured by the Germans in months of nibbling.

On the 26th Hindenburg sent his ultimatum to the
Chancellor, a blunt warning that he intended to have

his own way, and thereafter the decision taken by the military chiefs was covered by obtaining the Kaiser's formal agreement. How this was stage-managed is shown in a message sent by the Secretary at Pless: "His Majesty has received a large number of telegrams of assent and devotion in reply to his proclamation to the German people. In strict confidence, I hear that Field-Marshal von Hindenburg and General Ludendorff are responsible for a great number of these. . . . His Majesty has expressed himself highly pleased at these marks of homage. Their widest publication in the Press would, in my humble opinion, cause His Majesty much pleasure."

On February 1st, the unrestricted campaign was proclaimed. The possibility that it would invite American intervention had been weighed, but underweighed. The addition to the enemy's strength was lightly discounted in the assurance of early victory before it could affect the balance.

7. CHANGES AT THE HELM

The decision to embark on "absolute war" at sea, ruthlessly brushing aside the protests of the statesmen as well as their peace projects, showed that in Germany the military power was paramount. Hitherto the political power had been allowed to keep a hand at the helm; now it was under the hand of the martial helmsman—who was steering the ship of State into a perilous channel and then, in the blind pride of

his caste tradition, would run it onto the rocks rather
than accept inglorious salvage.

Among the opposing peoples there were signs of an
opposite tendency. The weakness of democracy for
war was also its strength. Inefficiency was the price
paid by the democracies for their political system:
vitality was the value they derived from it. They were
more likely to bend but less likely to break—because
they had elasticity and because they could break the
grip of a dead hand on the helm.

In France, the memory of a past tradition had revived so strongly in crisis as to produce for a time the
spectacle of Governments curiously subservient to the
military power. Popular impatience found vent in a
frequent change of Government. Joffre stayed on. After two years of war he was the only commander
among any of the great antagonists who had kept his
place. But he fell at last when 1916 drew to a close,
after vainly sacrificing his assistants to postpone his
end. A jaded people thirsting for a leader who promised something better than interminable attrition, followed the scent of the two recent ripostes at Verdun.
The army commander who had carried them through
was Nivelle. The very freshness of his fame quickly
gave his name a magic sound. He was called to be
Joffre's successor.

The British people had already tried a change of
command, and the Somme did not suggest that it was
a quick remedy. Their Government had been re-
shuffled in May 1915 when the first outburst of public
dissatisfaction had led the Liberal Prime Minister,

Mr. Asquith, to quench it by the inclusion of his political opponents in the Government. In this Coalition the Conservative element acquired a preponderant voice, save that the dynamic personality of Lloyd George gave him an increasing individual influence. But as time passed while prospects steadily faded, the cause was more and more generally identified with the continued presence of the original Prime Minister— the man who to a criticism had retorted "Wait and see," a reply which was remembered and given a wider meaning, as waiting failed to bring a change of outlook, save for the worse.

If depression deepened, exasperation heightened— and proved the stronger force. Discussions, arranged by Lord Beaverbrook, between Bonar Law, the Conservative leader, Carson, the Ulster leader, and Lloyd George, culminated in a proposal for a committee of three to run the war under the Prime Minister's direction. Asquith accepted the proposal; then became suspicious, and threw it in the melting-pot by a decision to reconstruct the Government on his own lines. This led to Lloyd George's resignation, and Asquith followed. The King then summoned Bonar Law, who suggested that a National Government should be formed under Balfour. Asquith refused to take a secondary place in any Government, whether under Balfour or Bonar Law. Lloyd George was then called on, and succeeded in forming a Government through the support of Bonar Law and Balfour.

Lloyd George replaced the large Cabinet of tradition by a small War Cabinet composed of Ministers who were free from departmental cares and could thus give their whole thought to the problems of directing the war as a whole. The five original members were, besides the Prime Minister, Bonar Law, Lord Curzon, Lord Milner, and Mr. Arthur Henderson. Later, leading representatives of the Dominions took part in its discussions from time to time. New Ministries were set up to control shipping, food supplies and man-power. The new War Cabinet system came close to being dictatorship within democracy—fulfilling the needs of efficiency without sacrificing the right to discussion. Owing to the breach in the Liberal Party, Lloyd George's position was weaker than it appeared on the surface because of his personal dependence on the Conservative element, which, apart from its chief leaders, tended to have the instinctive conviction that in war the soldier and sailor in authority must always be right. This produced in practice a definite limitation of the War Cabinet's powers in a most important sphere. It drove Lloyd George to seek his ends by ways that became more devious as the undercurrents of resistance and hostile intrigue became stronger, thus losing much of the time-saving advantages which the new organ promised. It was manifested early in the pursuit of such an obvious necessity as the attainment of unity of direction.

1917

1. THE ALLIES' MILITARY PLAN
FOR 1917

At the opening of the New Year a conference of the Allied leaders, political and military, was held in Rome to discuss the whole war situation. Its outlook, however, was already narrowed and its practical possibilities fettered by the purely military conference which Joffre had held at Chantilly in November before his fall. There Joffre had revealed that France no longer had sufficient men of military age to replace her losses; that her strength would be on the ebb during the coming year; and that the most the Allies could hope for in a renewed attempt to win victory in the west was a superiority of three to two. Yet he had inconsequently affrmed that the situation of the Allies was more favourable than it had ever been.

When Cadorna suggested that in the circumstances the French and British might find it more profitable to help in a combined effort on the Italian front to knock Austria out of the war, he was one against two —two minds on the Western Front that had but a single thought on the main issue—and his proposal was rejected. Joffre and Haig were intent on resuming their offensive on the Somme. Joffre intending thereafter to limit his expenditure and leave the main effort to the British, which Haig was ready to accept, being no less intent to fulfil his idea of a great offensive in Flanders—"the scheme," he wrote in his diary, "at which I have aimed for the past twelve months." Plans for this were set on foot in December and Haig insisted that they should aim at a swift "break-through."

These designs and desires governed the proceedings of the Rome conference. When Lloyd George took up the case for Cadorna's proposal, Briand, the French Prime Minister, pinned his faith to Nivelle's assurance that it was possible to break through the Western Front, and urged "the importance of not unsettling the military plans which were now far advanced." More surprisingly, Cadorna refrained from backing his own proposal, apparently moved by a sense of loyalty to his French and British soldier-colleagues.

If this sufficed to ensure that France and Britain devoted themselves to yet another great attempt to break through in the west, the common front began to crack when Nivelle and Haig came to settle their combined plan.

2. THE SPRING OFFENSIVE IN THE WEST 1917

Nivelle had succeeded not only to Joffre's place but to visions Joffre had gradually shed. He was confident of achieving a decisive break-through, and desired that France should play the leading role in it. The French Army therefore would deliver the main blow, in Champagne, as soon as the preparatory attacks north and south of the Somme had served their purpose of fixing the enemy's attention and reserves. Nivelle's plan had some advantage over Joffre's—at the time it was devised. The preparatory attacks would avoid the wilderness of the old Somme battlefields and instead be delivered on either side of it. The main blow in Champagne might profit by the fact that the German defensive system here was shallow, and the German reserves few. But the aggrandizement of the plan delayed its execution. And there were other causes of delay.

Haig appreciated the advantages of Nivelle's plan over Joffre's—not least because it promised a stronger effort by the French. Moreover, the reduction of the scale of the preparatory attack promised to release more British troops for his intended offensive in Flanders. But when Nivelle, in return, asked him to take over more of the French front, in order to release troops for the Champagne attack, Haig saw that this might, after all, curtail his own Flanders plan. His reluctance irritated Nivelle, who, feeling that there was no time to lose, appealed through his Government to the British Government. As a result a conference was called in mid-January. Here Haig suggested waiting for the promised Russian and Italian attacks in May, but it was decided that the offensive should be launched not later than April 1st—an inauspicious date! It was also settled that Haig should relieve the French south of the Somme and he was promised additional troops from England for the purpose.

The personal difficulties grew as the others were overcome. The French soldiers complained of Haig's obstructiveness, and the British of Nivelle's high-handedness. The tension was magnified by Haig's dissatisfaction with the French railway service, and he now took his turn in appealing to his own Government. This led to a fresh conference at Calais on February 26th. Here the French Staff reported by springing an unpalatable surprise on him—producing a scheme whereby the British armies would be placed under Nivelle's direction, his orders being issued to them through a British Chief of Staff at his headquarters. The idea violated a well-tested principle that a general cannot effectively direct another force while exercising executive command of his own.

But Lloyd George, in his desire for unity of direction and his impatience with what seemed the time-wasting wrangles of the two commands, seems to have inclined too readily to a compromise which could only have been workable under conditions of unusual goodwill and dispassionateness. Haig and Robertson were horrified at the French proposal and naturally resented the way it had been sprung on them. They agreed, in Haig's words, that they "would rather be tried by court martial than betray the army by agreeing to its being placed under the French." Although they were offered a good ground of objection on the score of military principle, at the time they seem to have overlooked it. Haig's diary shows that he concentrated on the "national" argument, saying that "it would be madness to place the British forces under the French, and that I did not believe our troops would fight under French leadership."

After heated discussion, a compromise was reached by which Haig agreed to act under Nivelle's strategic direction during the forthcoming offensive but with the right of appeal. But suspicions had been quickened, and feelings left raw. The day after signing this agreement, Haig took offence at the rather peremptory tone of a letter of instructions which Nivelle sent him, and was moved to exercise his right of appeal. He decided to send it to the Cabinet with "a request to be told, whether it is their wishes that the Commander-in-Chief of their British Army should be subjected to such treatment by a junior *foreign* commander." The reference to "junior" needs to be explained: Haig had now been made a field-marshal whereas Nivelle, the senior in years, was a general of division, this being the highest normal grade in the French Army. The idea of laying such emphasis on a nominal difference of rank between the heads of two armies which had a different system of grading may seem to show a lack of proportion, but it is important to appreciate it if one is to understand the subconscious working of the military mind.

Haig's protest reopened the whole issue. Nivelle felt that Haig was evading the agreement, and he was supported by the French Government. Nivelle's staff began a private agitation for Haig's removal. Haig, on his side, was fortified by a private letter from Lord Derby, the Secretary of State for War, and even more by the fact that the King was "very outspoken in his determination to 'support me through thick and thin'." He had also had time to prepare a carefully weighed statement of his case, concentrating on the need for a clearer definition of Nivelle's powers under the agreement.

At a fresh conference in London on March 12th Lloyd George induced the French to forgo some of their demands and Haig to modify some of his objections. Some further safeguards were included in the agreement but the argument turned more on the form than on the substance of Nivelle's instructions. A settlement was reached, and a personal talk between the two commanders soon afterwards did even more to allay the trouble.

But by now the Germans had intervened, upsetting the foundations of Nivelle's plan. On taking charge, Ludendorff had set out to reorganize and develop the German war-machine, and meantime he intended to abstain from attack, waiting to see whether the submarine campaign proved decisive. Anticipating a renewal of the Allied offensive on the Somme, he decided to forestall it by falling back to a new line of defence, immensely strong, which was rapidly constructed across the base of the great salient formed by the German front between Arras and Reims. To make his strategic retirement more effective, he decided to present the Allies with a desert: on the evacuated area roads were mined, trees cut down, wells fouled, and houses demolished, the ruins being strewn with explosive booby-traps. After a preliminary step back on February 23rd, the main withdrawal was quickly and smoothly made on March 16th. It dislocated Nivelle's plan—the more completely because the Allied chiefs were slow to believe that any soldier would willingly abandon occupied ground, however valueless.

The day after the Germans' preliminary move Robertson informed Nivelle that it was evident that the Germans intended to maintain their position intact and on March 4th Nivelle replied that he shared his views, being confident that the short retirement was not the beginning of a more extended withdrawal. Although Haig came to have doubts, Nivelle was slow to share them. When he was at last convinced that the Germans were retiring, he declared that "if he had whispered orders to Hindenburg, the latter could not have better executed what he desired."

This reasoning did not impress the men who had to execute the attack under conditions now compli cated by the German retirement. Their confidence had already been weakened by Nivelle's casual uncon· cern with the difficulties of fulfilling, with a mass of three armies, an operation which he airily described as "Laon in twenty-fours hours and then the pursuit." When Micheler, the army group commander, informed him in the middle of February that the Germans were completing in Champagne a third line out of reach of the French artillery, Nivelle exclaimed: "Don't be anxious, you won't find a German in those trenches, they only want to be off!" Then came the dislocation of the French plans by the German withdrawal from part of the threatened front: Micheler himself suggested that it would be wiser to stand on the defensive in France and send troops to Italy, to gain a victory there before the Germans did so. But

Nivelle was not to be deterred and simply said: "You won't find any Germans in front of you." Almost all the responsible commanders now doubted the sanity of Nivelle's calculations, but their opposition merely drove him to a frenzy of vaunting prediction. He declared that he would break through "with insignificant loss," and that in three days at most his armies would be sweeping through open country on their way to the Rhine. Painlevé, the new War Minister, vainly tried to persuade him to heed the doubts of his generals, but Nivelle got his way by threatening resignation. The Government feared the effect on public opinion too much to take the risk of accepting it.

The Germans were less perturbed than Nivelle's own subordinates by the threat of his attack. By the time it came they increased their original ten divisions on the chosen sector to forty-three—so that the French attack had bare equality of strength. There is a suspicion that some of Nivelle's critics took a less honest method than open protest of checking his aims, for on April 4th a mere sergeant-major who fell into the Germans' hands was found to have in his possession plans which clearly indicated the action and objectives of the several corps of the Fifth Army. But Nivelle himself had broadcast his intentions so freely and flamboyantly that the Germans had already been given ample warning.

The British opened the ball on April 9th with an attack by Allenby's Third Army at Arras, launched in a series of snowstorms. This began well, thanks to much improved artillery methods and a new gas-shell which paralysed the hostile artillery; thanks, also, to the delusions of the opposing Army Commander which partly offset the three weeks' notice given him by the obvious British preparations. Vimy Ridge, the scene of so many vain French offensives, fell to the attack of the Canadian corps. But the exploitation of the success, which had shaken the nerve of the opposing command, was frustrated—largely through the congestion of the traffic arteries behind the British front, a congestion increased by moving up masses of cavalry who became a target for the enemy's guns. Thenceforward the British butted at a hardening resistance, steadily increasing their loss without compensating profit.

Nivelle's own offensive in Champagne on April 16th proved a tragic fiasco. By nightfall the French had advanced about six hundred yards instead of the six miles anticipated in Nivelle's programme. The attacking troops were trapped in a web of machine-gun fire. The French Senegalese troops broke and fled, even storming hospital trains in their anxiety to get away. Only on the wings was any appreciable progress achieved. The results compared favourably with Joffre's offensives for some 28,000 prisoners were taken at a cost to the French of just under 120,000 casualties. But the effect was worse, because Nivelle's fantastic prophecies were more widely known than Joffre's had been. With the collapse of Nivelle's plan, his fortunes were buried in the ruins, and after some face-saving delay Pétain succeeded him on May 15th.

This change was made too late to avert a more

harmful sequel, for on May 3rd a mutiny broke out and spread until sixteen army corps were affected. The authorities chose to ascribe it to seditious propaganda, but the outbreaks always occurred when exhausted troops were ordered back into the line, and were accompanied by such significant cries as: "We'll defend the trenches, but we won't attack." Pétain restored tranquillity by meeting the just grievances of the troops; he restored confidence by his reputation for sober judgment and for avoiding reckless attacks. But the military strength of France could never be fully restored. Nivelle had completed Joffre's work too well.

Pétain insisted that the only rational strategy was to keep to the defensive until new factors had changed the conditions sufficiently to justify taking the offensive with a reasonable hope of success. His constant advice was: "We must wait for the Americans and the tanks." The latter were now being belatedly built in large numbers, and this emphasis upon them showed a dawning recognition that machine-warfare had superseded mass-warfare. The Americans were a reinforcement now assured by action which sprung from the narrowly military outlook of German leadership.

3. AMERICA'S ENTRY

For two and a half years President Wilson had steadfastly held to his neutral policy, undeflected by his own sympathies or by taunts, or by concrete provocation. Meantime, he strove, with the aid of his trusted adviser and envoy, Colonel House, to find a basis of peace upon which the warring countries could agree. The effort was foredoomed because reason was submerged by emotion, the people in the grip of their passions, while the fighting men, most of whom had shed such feelings, were in the grip of the war-machines. The President's chances of persuading the Allied peoples were hindered by the fact that, carrying neutrality into the realm of moral judgment, he seemed not to recognize any distinction between the aggressor and the victim. If this attitude cloaked his real convictions, and was a necessity in a would-be mediator, it naturally infuriated those who believed themselves to be fighting the battle for liberty. On the other hand, his chances of securing the attention of Germany were nullified because those who were in a mood to listen were now more helplessly than ever in the grip of a military regime which scorned all con·cessions not won by conquest.

The reception of his peace endeavours hardened the President's tendency to classify all the belligerents alike as naughty schoolboys. While the repulse did not shake his confidence in ultimately securing peace by mediation it deepened his determination to persist in neutrality. In November he had won re-election on the claim that he had kept the United States out of the war, and early in the New Year he declared privately his resolve: "This country does not intend to become involved in war."

A few weeks later the declaration of the German submarine campaign, and its accompanying repudiation of the pledges formerly given to him, sealed the fate of his peace-moves and showed the futility of his hopes. He at once severed diplomatic relations, but still clung to the belief that Germany's actions would stay short of her threats. That belief was soon falsified by the sinking of several American ships. Then a telegram was intercepted and deciphered which showed that Germany had the intention of inciting Mexico to action against the United States, with the promise of New Mexico, Texas and Arizona, and with the hope of gaining Japan's adherence to this plan. More sinkings followed—and at last the President conquered his hesitations. On April 6th America entered the war against Germany.

The news was a great moral tonic to the Allies and became greater as the months brought them, otherwise, growing cause for gloom. But the President had carried his devotion to neutrality so far as to abstain, despite House's promptings, from any serious preparations against the risk of having to change his policy. Everything had to be improvised in haste, and the scale of the improvisation ensured confusion in the process. The existing American Army, as General Peyton March has pointed out "was of no practical military value" for participation in a European War. General Pershing has recorded that it had in reserve only 550 guns, only enough shells to provide a nine hours' bombardment even with the limited number of guns, only fifty-five aeroplanes—of which fifty-one were graded as obsolete and the other four as obsolescent. The Navy was in better state, but the expansion agreed upon in the previous August was far short of achievement.

For some time America's aid apart from its purely moral effect, could only be a promissory note except in the economic sphere. And even here the difficulty of grasping the cost of waging war proved a check for some months. By July 1917, Britain had spent over £5,000,000,000 and her daily expenditure was no less than £7,000,000. Her resources were being gravely strained by the burden of financing her Allies as well as her own efforts. She had lent £900,000,000 by the time America entered the war. Unused to such an aspect of war, Congress was aghast at the appeals for loans which came from Europe, and tried to restrict the flow.

After three months of war the Government had made advances totalling £229,000,000, with the restriction that this was to be used in payment for supplies bought in the United States. Britain in the same period had added £193,000,000 to her loans, without any such restriction. On top of this fresh strain came the danger of having to sell securities with consequent damage to British credit. Balfour was so alarmed that he cabled to House: "We seem to be on the verge of a financial disaster which would be worse than defeat in the field. If we cannot keep up our exchange neither we nor our Allies can pay our dollar debts. We should be driven off the gold basis, and purchases from the U.S.A. would immediately cease and the Allies' credit would be shattered." Overriding opposition, the United States Treasury took measures to meet the emergency and before long advances to the Allies were authorized up to $500,000,000 a month. By the end of the year the problem had changed. For owing to the vast needs of America's own forces, the difficulty of the Allies was to obtain the supplies for whose purchase they had been given credit.

One other important effect of America's entry in the Allied cause was the way it enabled the economic grip on Germany to be tightened with strangling effect, regardless of protests from the remaining neutrals. As Mr. Polk half humorously said to Balfour in Washington: "It took Great Britain three years to reach a point where it was prepared to violate all the laws of blockade. You will find it will take us only two months to become as great criminals as you are." The United States, indeed, showed the utmost determination in enforcing and extending the measures against which they had formerly protested so strenuously. At the same time, the increasing reinforcement of their light craft helped to counteract the German submarine blockade, already past its height—which was reached in the very month that America entered the war.

4. THE SUBMARINE CAMPAIGN

In April 1917, one ship out of every four which left the British Isles never came home. The Allies lost nearly a million tons of shipping, sixty per cent of it British, during that month when the sinkings reached their peak. The largest part of it was lost in the approaches to the English Channel and the Irish Sea, which became a maritime cemetery. Yet only five or six submarines, on an average, were operating in this area at any one time during these months. The direct loss of food and raw materials was increased by the growing hesitation of neutral shipping to take the risk of supplying an island whose approaches were so perilous. The German Staff had counted on this frightening effect, as well as on the sinking of 600,000 tons of shipping a month, when formulating their conclusion that "an unrestricted U-boat war, started at the proper time, will bring about peace before the harvesting period of the 1917 summer, that is before August 1st."

The British Admiralty estimates agreed with these ominous predictions. Unless some drastic change could be achieved, the starvation of Britain and the collapse of her armed effort was in sight. Only the fibre of her merchant-seamen preserved her—theirs was the cold courage of men who were performing their job, without any stimulus of martial enthusiasm or emotional appeal. The Government pressed on with the expansion of shipbuilding, the rationing of food, and the increase of home production. But the danger was growing more rapidly. In vain, the Navy multiplied the means of combating the submarine: 3000 destroyers and light craft were devoted to the task, aided by new devices to detect the presence of the hidden foe. The results were petty compared with the effort. There was one method still untried, the most obvious method of all—that of bringing the ships to port in convoy. But the Admiralty had a fixed professional opinion that convoy was theoretically unsound; and this opinion, like all doctrinal beliefs, was hard to shake, growing stiffer the more the idea was urged from outside.

When Lloyd George, faced with the Admiralty's spirit of blank resignation to fate, mooted the possibility of trying convoy at a conference on November 2nd, 1916, Jellicoe declared that "they would never be able to keep merchant ships sufficiently together to enable a few destroyers to screen them." The First Sea Lord, Sir Henry Jackson, had stated that in any case it would be impossible to "protect by escort even a small proportion of the sailings." Admiral Duff, the Director of the Anti-Submarine Division, found numerous arguments to show the impracticability of the idea. So the months passed, while the prospect grew worse. There were younger officers, notably Commander Henderson, who believed in convoy, and in February Hankey reinforced their persuasive efforts by a memorandum in which he pointed out, with logic, that "Perhaps the best commentary on the convoy system is that it is invariably adopted for our main fleet, and for our transports."

But enthroned authority stood firm against such logic, and was unwilling to put it to an experimental test. To show the impossibility of providing sufficient escort, figures were actually given which demonstrated that there were 2500 voyages a week each way. It was Commander Henderson who, baulked of information at the Admiralty, eventually investigated the facts with the aid of the Ministry of Shipping. It was found, as the Official Naval History says, that the figures "had been made to include the repeated calls of coasters and shortsea traders." The actual arrivals and departures in the ocean trade were less than 140 a week.

Yet, even when America entered the war, Jellicoe, who had become First Sea Lord, still opposed convoy, asserting that he had not enough destroyers. On April 9th Admiral Sims reached London and saw Jellicoe who showed him the list of sinkings and told him: "It is impossible for us to go on with the war if losses like this continue." When Sims asked if he had found any solution to the problem, Jellicoe replied: "Absolutely none that we can see now." These words are borne out by Jellicoe's gloomy memorandum at the end of the month: "We are carrying on the war at the present time as if we had absolute command of the sea, whereas we have not such command or anything approaching it." To be masters of the surface was "quite useless if the enemy's submarines paralyse, as they do now, our lines of communication." We were *heading straight for disaster.*

It was Lloyd George who now made the decisive intervention, visiting the Admiralty and warning them beforehand that he intended to consult any officers he wished, irrespective of rank. He found the Board now willing to try the experiment which they had hitherto opposed. The first convoy left Gibraltar on May 10th, and a transatlantic convoy proved equally successful at the end of the month. Even then, the Prime Minister had to intervene once more before the Admiralty adopted the practice as a regular system.

The results gave to this trial of common sense a magical air. By September the British loss of shipping had fallen to 200,000 tons a month, while the loss in the convoys was reduced to a bare one per cent. Meantime the counter-offensive campaign was reinforced by special submarine-chasers, aircraft, and the new horned mines: these exacted an ever-rising toll of submarines. By the end of the year the menace was largely subdued and the danger past.

5. THE PASSCHENDAELE OFFENSIVE

The Admiralty's attitude was to have a fateful reaction on the Army. Jellicoe's pessimism, blended with Haig's optimism, and with the obstinate adherence to preconceived theories which so often accompanies professional ability, produced a mixture fatal to multitudes of British soldiers. The British cause itself was endangered by the after-effects.

The collapse of Nivelle's castle-in-the-air had an effect on Haig the reverse of that on Pétain. While Pétain at once manifested his intention of staying on the defensive until the Americans arrived, Haig was spurred to an attempt to win the war by British arms before the Americans could arrive. The relapse of the French into a secondary and passive role was an opportunity to play his own hand without being hampered by a partner's lead. Free at last of the irksome need of conforming to the French plans, he could now fulfil his long-cherished desire for an offensive in Flanders. He seized the chance with as much eagerness as a reserved Lowland Scot could show. "I think the time has nearly come for me to take up our 'alternative plan' in earnest." The more he contemplated "our plan" the more rosy his picture grew. It became a vision of victory, a victory so decisive that it would end the war. He so far forgot his natural caution on paper that even in an official memorandum he expressed the "considered opinion" that a British offensive could be "relied on to effect great results this summer," and "might quite possibly lead to their (the Germans') collapse."

In later years, when that dream had been dispelled and "Passchendaele" had become a name of ill-fame, Haig was wont to argue that his dominant motive in pressing on with that offensive had been to take pressure off his Allies—"the possibility of the French Army breaking up *compelled me to go on attacking.*" It would seem that by 1927 he had come, by oft-reiteration, to believe this explanation of his own motive in 1917. Nothing has come to light that shows the existence of such a thought. On the contrary, letters of his at the time, as well as the evidence of some of his chief assistants, show clearly that he was filled with the idea that it was possible for the British Army to defeat the Germans single-handed "at an early date." Far from being shaken in this belief by two months of hard experience, with his army deeper in the mud, he became more confident than ever that he was on the verge of a decisive victory. Far from emphasizing

the weakness of the French as a reason for pressing his
effort, he asserted that the French were more than
capable of holding their own; that they were "fully
equal to an equivalent number" of Germans, and
were preventing the Germans from moving troops to
resist him—thus increasing his opportunity. He was
assured, in September, that "the morale of the French
troops is now excellent."

At no time during 1917 were there any serious signs
of a German offensive against the French, and we
know now that the Germans never contemplated any
such attack. Indeed, they were thinking of a withdrawal to stave off the danger of a French attack. Like Pétain, and unlike Haig, they had come with experience
to the resolve not to attempt the offensive until conditions were favourable. Meantime they were impressed by the fact that at Verdun in August "the
French had fought very vigorously."

We know, too, that both Pétain and Foch (who had
now become head of the French General Staff) doubted the wisdom of Haig's effort, questioning both its
site and its method. According to Wilson's diary, Pétain expressed the opinion as early as May 19th that
"Haig's attack towards Ostend was certain to fail,"
and on June 2nd Foch declared that "the whole thing
was futile, fantastic and dangerous." Yet a few weeks
later Wilson was lending his voice to persuade the
War Cabinet to agree to Haig's plans—which at least
suggests that he had no strong personal objection to
them. But even if a doubt should remain on this score,
the authenticity of Pétain's and Foch's doubts is con-

firmed by other British liaison officers with the French
—and by Pétain himself. "To excuse Marshal Haig,"
he answered an enquiry from the British Prime Minister with the cryptic comment that, "One doesn't
fight the Germans and the mud simultaneously." Pétain was glad of any help that Haig could offer, but he
preferred it to be in the form of taking over more of
the French line. Although he fell in with Haig's plan,
since British troops were bearing the main cost, he did
not care for the idea that his Allies might exhaust
themselves prematurely—by adopting methods that
were contrary to his deepest convictions.

After the failure of Nivelle's offensive an inter-
allied conference had been held in Paris on May 4th.
Here Lloyd George sought to put heart into the
French Government, urging them to continue their
efforts, while impressing on them the uselessness of
the British continuing to attack if the French ceased.
An agreement was reached on this point. But as the
Australian Official History remarks: "The agreement
was only apparent. To Pétain—and Robertson was to
a large extent in agreement with him—the project
meant the employment of a new, restricted, but certain method of wearing-down the enemy at the small-
est possible cost to the attacking troops. . . . To Haig
the agreement means something quite different—permission to prepare for the Flanders offensive . . . with
an aim which went far beyond the mere wearing-down
of the enemy's strength."

Within a few days his troops were on the move to
Flanders, where preparations had been "continued

steadily" since the beginning of the year. Haig did not
regard his offensive as dependent on the French continuing to attack. He had already told his Army Commanders privately that he did not expect much from
the French. But when the War Cabinet expressed
similar doubts to his own, and questioned the wisdom
of launching the British offensive without such aid,
Haig assured them that the French attacks would be
on an adequate scale. Yet in the interval Pétain had
told him that he could promise nothing more than
two limited attacks, at Verdun and in Champagne.
Robertson had also warned Haig of the importance of
economizing his strength, saying that he "must not expect many men as drafts," because of agricultural and
industrial needs.

Haig's plan embraced a preliminary attack on the
Messines Ridge, in order to straighten out the Ypres
salient and attract the enemy's reserves. This was executed on June 7th by the Second Army under Plumer.
A strictly limited attack, made on true siege-war methods and based on preparations begun a year before, it
proved an almost complete success within its limits. It
owed much to the surprise-effect of nineteen huge
mines, simultaneously fired, if still more to the folly of
the German corps commanders who refused to listen
to suggestions that they should forestall the suspected
blow by a withdrawal, and even insisted on keeping
their troops packed in the forward position, ready to
be blown up.

This success had the unfortunate effect of inspiring
the higher command with too much confidence in the

greater effort that was to follow, wherein the methods were essentially different. When Haig discussed with the two Army Commanders, Gough and Plumer, what objective they should fix for the first day of this offensive, Gough, like Haig's own Operations Staff, favoured the idea of a step-by-step method, but Plumer urged that they should "go all out." Haig agreed with him—although Plumer was taking the smaller share in the offensive. Haig counted on an early breakthrough, if not at the first thrust. He told his Army Commanders that "opportunities for the employment of cavalry in masses are likely to offer."

There was cause to doubt this, as well as the possibility of a rapid advance even by the infantry. General Headquarters had information, collected by the Engineer Staff two years before and again by the Tank Corps Staff now, which indicated that the Ypres area, being reclaimed marshland, was bound to revert to swamp if the drainage system were to be destroyed by prolonged bombardment. In addition, according to the head of Haig's Intelligence Staff, "Careful investigation of the records of more than eighty years showed that in Flanders the weather broke early each August with the regularity of the Indian monsoon: once the autumn rains set in the difficulties would be greatly enhanced."

None of these facts were disclosed by Haig to the War Cabinet when he went over to London late in June to secure their approval of his plans. He began by dwelling on the "exhaustion" of the German Army and its declining morale. The War Cabinet expressed anxiety whether so great an operation would not cause heavy casualties, which would be difficult to replace in the present state of man-power. Haig replied that he thought there was no ground for such fears. In closing the meeting, the Prime Minister said that while he appreciated Haig's point of view, "the Committee must consider whether it would not be better to hold out until the French Army had been resuscitated by the intervention of America."

Before the next day's meeting the Prime Minister set down, for the attention of Haig and Robertson, a number of arguments against the plan. He remarked that "a great attack which fails in its objective while entailing heavy casualties must necessarily discourage the British Army," besides having a grave effect "upon public opinion in Britain and France." "The Cabinet must regard themselves as trustees" for the men who constituted the Army, and must see that they were "not sacrificed on mere gambles." It was impossible to take more men from agriculture and shipbuilding while the submarine menace remained, and difficult to take them from the mines and factories without risk of strikes that would entail a loss of war material. The chances of success were dubious—the Germans had the superiority in reserves, and "something like equality" in other respects: "Even if the French Army pulls its full weight, the Allies can only command a bare superiority on the Western Front. If it pulls less than its full weight we shall be attacking the strongest army in the world, entrenched in the most formidable positions with an actual inferiority of numbers. I do not pretend to know anything about the rules of strategy, but curious indeed must be the military conscience which could justify an attack under such conditions." In face of reports received about the state of the French Army they could not this year rely upon it "to take its full part in such an enterprise." The Prime Minister then discussed alternatives, favouring an offensive against Austria. He pointed out that the Italians had a great superiority in men over the Austrians. "What they lack is guns and ammunition; these we can supply."

When the meeting was resumed next day, Robertson expressed himself as "sceptical" of the Austrian alternative. He "deprecated as strongly as anyone our incurring heavy casualties without corresponding return, but the plan as outlined by the Field-Marshal should secure us against this mistake." Haig said that he was "fully in agreement with the Committee that we ought not to push attacks that had not a reasonable chance of success, but that we ought to proceed step by step." He himself had "no intention of entering into a tremendous offensive involving heavy losses."

The War Cabinet still hesitated, but Jellicoe now came into the meeting and made a powerful intervention in favour of Haig's plan, saying that unless the Army could capture the submarine bases on the Belgian coast he considered it "improbable that we could go on with the war next year for lack of shipping."

Haig won his case—for fighting the battle that he would not win. On his return to France he told his Intelligence chief, General Charteris, of the struggle and of the decisive effect of Jellicoe's declaration. General Headquarters regarded this as "a rather amazing view," while appreciating the fact that it had "sufficient weight to make the Cabinet agree to our attack going on." Charteris, however, was a little dismayed to learn that Haig had gone beyond the general figures furnished by his Intelligence Staff and had given "the definite opinion that if the fighting was kept up at its present intensity for six months Germany would be at the end of her available man-power."

Preparations were now pressed forward—on both sides of the battle-front. For the German commanders were now agreed that a British offensive at Ypres was "certain," and its exact pattern was judged "with perfect accuracy." By July 6th, the Crown Prince Rupprecht, the German Army Group Commander, was satisfied that he now had ample troops and ammunition to meet the expected attack. On July 10th, he took by surprise the British bridge-head near the sea, and thus upset the coastal move which was intended to help Haig's frontal assault.

For an early break-through such as Haig was aiming at, surprise was of vital importance, but in choosing to attack in the bare Flanders plain all Haig's immense preparations were displayed to the eyes of the German observers. A fortnight's bombardment gave them further warning. As one of the official historians remarks, "No offensive—even including Nivelle's—was ever so clearly heralded or so confidently awaited."

The actual plan of advance was also a cause of serious doubt to the officers who had to carry it out. General Uikacke, the artillery adviser of the Fifth Army, pointed out that the intended front of attack would be dominated by the German artillery from the high ground on the right, while our own artillery would not have enough elbow room. To avoid this Gough asked, but without success, that Plumer's Army should take a full share in the attack. The truth of the Fifth Army's warning was soon proved. As Gough has remarked: "The more our left pushed forward, the deeper it became buried in a salient, and the enemy could bring a converging and enfilade fire to bear on us from the high ground opposite our right, instead of we on them as in 1916."

The offensive was launched on July 31st after over 3000 guns had poured four and half million shells on the German defences. They did not suffice to silence the hostile machine-guns, many of which were ensconced in concrete "pill-boxes." Only on the left was the full objective reached, and on the crucial right wing the attack was a failure. Yet Haig, in his report to the War Office on the first day's fighting, stated that the results were "most satisfactory." On August 4th Charteris had this diary note: "Every brook is swollen and the ground is a quagmire. If it were not that all the records of previous years had given us fair warning, it would seem as if Providence had declared against us."

The next big effort had to be postponed until the 16th and then proved a failure. Gough suggested that "the attack should be abandoned." Rawlinson also questioned the likelihood of the Germans' early breakdown, but Haig remained confident. On August 21st he told the Government that the end of their reserves was in sight, although the struggle might still be severe "for some weeks." Robertson now began to feel increasing doubts—but he did not disclose them to the Government, whose official adviser he was. A month later, telling Haig that he had "knocked out" alternative plans and was still backing Haig's, he added: "I confess I stick to it more because . . . my instinct prompts me to stick to it, than because of any good argument by which I can support it."

After repeated local attacks by Gough's troops had achieved practically nothing except loss to themselves, Haig agreed to Plumer's army taking an enlarged role. The method of attack had come to be questioned even in G.H.Q. itself; and a paper on the question led General Rawlinson to submit an appreciation in which he pointed out that "the British command had never yet attempted to conduct a wearing-down battle with planned, logical methods, but had relied too much on its belief that a breakdown of the German Army's morale was within sight." Haig was not impressed by these views, but his decision to extend Plumer's role fulfilled them indirectly. The preparations took several weeks and gave the troops some respite from vain sacrifice. As the Australian Official History remarks: "The truth was that these strokes, aimed at the morale of the German Army, were wearing down the morale of the British. Whether British commanders were aware of the facts or not, it was the August fighting that gave to the Third Battle of Ypres its baneful reputation. The fighting at Passchendaele two months later merely added to this." Rupprecht, who had often noted the resolute bearing of British prisoners, was shocked when one of them said that "they would gladly shoot down the officers who ordered them to attack." He learnt from his own infantry that the British now surrendered easily. If the German troops were also suffering, they were now "imbued with confidence" and Ludendorff had sufficient confidence to begin "preparations not only for attacking the Russians at Riga but for crushing the Italians by sending eight or ten divisions to assist the Austrians."

When the Prime Minister went over to Flanders, Haig laid great stress on the poor physique of the prisoners then being taken, as proof that his offensive was bringing the German Army to exhaustion. The Prime Minister asked to see one of the prisoners' cages; after being taken there he had to admit that the prisoners were a "weedy lot." Actually, however, a staff officer at G.H.Q. had telephoned to the Fifth Army, to warn them of the visit and to give instructions that "all ablebodied prisoners were removed from the corps cages" before his arrival.

In late September there was an improvement both in the weather and in the British situation. On the 20th, 26th, and again on October 4th, successful strokes of a strictly limited nature were delivered. The farthest objective on the 20th was less than a mile deep, and was reduced still more on the subsequent strokes. "The advancing barrage won the ground; the infantry merely occupied it." Plumer had one gun to every five yards of front, and this huge concentration of fire crushed the enemy's counter-attacks. The result, together with the better organization of the attack, helped to revive the spirit of the attacking troops.

The effect, however, proved too intoxicating behind the front. At a conference on September 28th Haig expressed his belief that the enemy were on the point of collapse, and that tanks and cavalry could be pushed through. Ten days later he told the Government that the breakdown of the enemy's resistance might come "at any moment." He had already told them that the German losses exceeded the British "not improbably by a hundred per cent"—they were, actually, much less than the British.

His assistants, both executive and advisory, became more and more dubious of his optimistic assurances, as the weather deteriorated and the mud became worse. But with military loyalty they tried to make their thoughts become the children of their wishes. On October 5th, Charteris admitted in a note: "Unless we get fine weather for all this month, there is no chance of clearing the coast. . . . Most of those at the conference would welcome a stop." Nevertheless, after two days' heavy rain, he remarked on October 8th: "With a great success to-morrow, and good weather for a few more weeks, we may still clear the coast and win the war before Christmas." That same day Harington, Plumer's Chief of Staff, declared at a conference that the crest of the ridge would be found—"as dry as a bone."

On October 10th Charteris made the note: "I was out all day yesterday at the attack. It was the saddest day of the year . . . there is now no chance of complete success here this year. . . . D.H. sent for me about 10 (p.m.) to discuss things. . . . He was still trying to find some grounds for hope that we might still win through here this year, but there is none."

A fresh attack was nevertheless ordered for the 12th with still deeper objectives. Gough tried to secure a postponement but without avail. This attack ended with the attacking troops, save those who had perished in the mud, back on their starting line. Fresh efforts were ordered, and made, on the 22nd, 26th, and 30th, "Very little progress was made." On November 6th, however, the troops advanced the few hundred yards necessary to occupy the site of what had been the village of Passchendaele, and Haig at last called a halt, with honour satisfied. He was in a practical sense no nearer reaching the ports that formed his goal than when he had started. His dream of a decisive victory had failed. The cost had been 400,000 men—a contrast to his pledge that he would not commit the country to "heavy losses." If such an effort had, naturally, imposed a severe strain on the enemy, they had felt it less than on the Somme. The strain on Haig's own forces had been greater even than on the Somme. The conditions in which they fought have been well described by the Army Commander who was there throughout:

"Many pens have tried to describe the ghastly expanse of mud which covered this waterlogged country, but few have been able to paint a picture sufficiently intense. Imagine a fertile countryside, dotted every few hundred yards with peasant farms and an occasional hamlet; water everywhere, for only an intricate system of small drainage canals relieved the land from the ever-present danger of flooding. . . . Then imagine this same countryside battered, beaten, and torn by a torrent of shell and explosive . . . such as no land in the world had yet witnessed—the soil shaken and re-shaken, fields tossed into new and fantastic shapes, roads blotted out from the landscape, houses and hamlets pounded into dust so thoroughly that no man could point to where they had stood, and the intensive and essential drainage system utterly and irretrievably destroyed. This alone presents a battle-ground of tremendous difficulty. But then came the incessant rain. The broken earth became a fluid clay; the little brooks and tiny canals became formidable obstacles, and every shell-hole a dismal pond; hills and valleys alike were but waves and troughs of a gigantic sea of mud. Still the guns churned this treacherous slime. Every day conditions grew worse. What had once been difficult now became impossible. The surplus water poured into the trenches as its natural outlet, and they became impassable for troops; nor was it possible to walk over the open field—men staggered warily over duck-board tracks. Wounded men falling headlong into the shell-holes were in danger of drowning. Mules slipped from the tracks and were often drowned in the giant shell-holes alongside. Guns sank till they became useless; rifles caked and would not fire; even food was tainted with the inevitable mud. No battle in history

was ever fought under such conditions as that of Passchendaele."

Shortly after the battle had been brought to a close,
one of Haig's principal coadjutors paid a visit to the
battle-front—his first visit. Growing increasingly uneasy as the car approached the fringe of the swamp-
like area, he was still well short of the real fighting line
when he burst into tears, crying: "Good God, did we
really send men to fight in that?"

6. THE BREAKDOWN IN ITALY

In Haig's survey of the war situation on October 8th,
his main arguments had been devoted to the value
of continuing the offensive in Flanders. In deference
to the Government he had considered various risks,
but only to dismiss them. He suggested that the Prime
Minister was being too pessimistic in imagining that
Russia might drop out; he indicated his own hopes
that she might continue to pin down at least as many
German divisions as hitherto. As for Italy, he treated
any danger to her as contingent on Russia's hypo-
thetical collapse, not as a present risk. Even if Russia
were to drop out, and Austria transfer all her strength
to the Italian front, "Italy should be able to hold her
ground unaided." He showed no recognition of the
danger that the Germans might deliver a stroke
against Italy.

Within less than three weeks the Italian front had
been broken by the thrust of a German spearhead, on

an Austrian shaft—although Haig's offensive was still maintained and Russia had not yet dropped out. Each autumn the Germans had seized the opportunity to demolish one of the weaker allies. Now it was to be Italy's turn.

Ludendorff's resolve was determined by appeals from war-weary Austria. In contrast to the scepticism of Haig and Robertson, her political and military chiefs were convinced that their ill-knit state was on the brink of collapse. The emergency was the more annoying to Ludendorff as he was preparing an offensive to consummate Russia's defeat. Able to spare only six divisions he sent a staff officer to search the Italian front for a "soft spot" where a comparatively small force might have the greatest effect. This was found in the Caporetto sector.

The attack was launched on October 24th in a thick fog intensified by snow and rain. It was preceded by only an hour's full bombardment. Nine Austrian divisions were combined with six German. A breakthrough was at once achieved. The Italian troops had been strained to the limit of their endurance by being pushed so often into vain attacks, and on this sector, despite warnings, were particularly weak. The breach quickly widened and the Italian front collapsed. Cadorna only saved the wreckage of his army by a hasty retreat, first to the Tagliamento, and then to the Piave —leaving over quarter of a million prisoners in the enemy's hands. He himself was replaced by General Diaz, who played a Pétain-like role in restoring confidence, helped likewise by an understanding of the

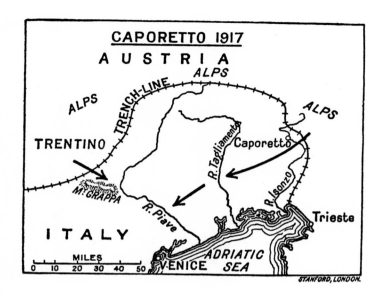

soldier's mind, which Cadorna, with his unbending ideas of discipline, had lacked.

Fortunately for the Italians the enemy had been surprised by the extent of their own success. Unwilling to stop short, they tried to push on without the resources or the communications necessary to maintain their momentum. The pursuit also suffered from internal friction between the German and Austrian commanders, and from the fact that to the ill-fed troops the well-filled Italian supply-depots proved a stronger attraction than the pursuit of glory. Thus the Italians were able to re-knit their line, and hold it, on the Piave—although they had lost 600,000 men.

Back in August Cadorna had made a fresh appeal for Allied help in an offensive, pointing out that at present his attacks were handicapped by lack of heavy artillery and ammunition. He begged for a minimum of 100 guns; 400, he suggested, were needed for a decisive effort. Foch had now come round, like other French generals earlier, to the opinion that it was "hopeless" to look for good results on the Western Front in 1917. Foch's support had strengthened Lloyd George's wish to meet Cadorna's appeal. But Robertson had refused to budge. Notwithstanding his own doubts of the Passchendaele offensive, he wrote to Haig frequently in the weeks that followed to assure him of his steadfastness in fighting Haig's battle, and to tell him how he had "knocked out" alternative projects.

Now in November the crisis in Italy forced Robertson and Haig to part with more troops to retrieve an

Italian disaster than had been asked for to make an Italian attack effective. And Italy's offensive power would be crippled for a year.

7. RUSSIA'S BREAK-AWAY

The disappearance of Russia from the war followed hard on the Italian disaster. At the end of 1916 the murder of the monk Rasputin, the hooded manipulator of royalty, released a surge of popular feeling which developed into a Revolution in March, 1917, and the Tsar was forced to abdicate. The long repressed hatred of a corrupt and inefficient regime had become merged in disgust with the war, producing a mixture so explosive that the moderate parties which first took over the Government had little chance of preserving a balance or their own hold. When passion takes charge, extremes win. In May, the Government was succeeded by another, more to the left. Its brilliantly emotional leader Kerensky, combined a cry of peace with platform appeals to the troops to carry on the war; he had neither the strength nor the span to achieve the difficult acrobatic feat of riding two horses at once. In July there was a fitful offensive against the Austrians, but it flickered out when the Germans counter-attacked. Hoffmann, who was now the directing brain on the Eastern Front, exploited the growing weakness of the Russians by a combination of strategy and policy. And the Russian reactionaries now intervened to seal their own fate, and that of the moderates by shaking the

Government which gave them shelter. Their attempted counter-revolution provided an opportunity to the Bolsheviks of the extreme left who, in November, overthrew Kerensky, and established their rule in Russia under the direction of Lenin and Trotsky, who combined dynamic force of character with a masterly grasp of the technique of revolution. They speedily sought an armistice with Germany, which was concluded in December.

The peace negotiations were prolonged until March, when an unopposed invasion forced acceptance of the Germans' drastic terms. The German statesmen would have been content to accept the fact of Russia's collapse, but the military leaders insisted on pursuing the fiction of her submission. What they gained by this martial threat was illusory, while it had the military disadvantage of hindering the despatch of forces to the Western Front. Nevertheless, the flow of reinforcements to the West from November onwards was large —thirty divisions had gone thither by the beginning of March to add to the 150 present there. A further twenty were released later.

8. THE HALF BREAK-THROUGH AT CAMBRAI

Before these reserves arrived there was a moment when a vista of victory opened before Haig's eyes —through a new agent. But it was not at the spot he had imagined, and the chance came too late. The resources needed to exploit it had been sunk in the swamps of Passchendaele.

As far back as August 3rd the Tank Corps staff had drafted a paper in which, after remarking that the futility of the Flanders offensive was already clear, they offered the alternative proposal of trying, as a diversion, a great tank raid. The dry downland near Cambrai was suggested as a suitable spot. The idea appealed to General Byng, the Commander of the Third Army, when it was broached to him. His picture of it grew: from a great raid into a great attack, leading to a great break-through by his army. The inflation of the idea endangered its prospects. For when Byng had discussed the project at G.H.Q., although Haig was inclined to favour it his Chief of Staff promptly objected that it contravened the principle of concentration at the decisive spot—Ypres. As a result the scheme was dropped while the offensive in Flanders continued. Not until the middle of October did the fading prospects of the Passchendaele campaign lead to its revival. Because of his reduced resources Haig only contemplated a limited aim: but Byng, given his chance, gave his plan an unbounded scope. Into the initial attack he threw all his divisions and all his tanks, leaving himself without reserves of either.

On November 20th, in a thick morning mist, 380 tanks rolled forward before a gun had opened fire. Six divisions joined in the attack, on a six-mile front. The absence of the customary bombardment took the Germans by surprise, and the deep trenches of the Hindenburg line were quickly breached. Only at one point, Flesquières, was there a serious check, due largely to a divisional commander who, having previously condemned the idea as "a fantastic and most unmilitary plan," now insisted on altering the formation which the tank experts had devised. But this was only an islet, lapped by waves which had penetrated five miles deep—further than had been attained in months of struggle on the Somme and in Flanders.

Three defence lines had been overrun, and only a half-finished line separated the British from open country. The Germans have recorded that there was a wide gap for "many hours, completely unoccupied." But the tanks had all been used, their crews were exhausted, the infantry were unable to make progress without them, and the cavalry, as usual, proved incapable of exploiting their chance—being easily stopped by a few machine-guns. Thus time was gained for German reserves to cement the breach. After forty-eight hours had passed, Haig decided to revoke his own time-limit, and belatedly sent a few fresh divisions. The French had placed an army corps at his disposal before the attack opened, but after the first day they had been told that they were not needed. The renewed British attacks on the 22nd and 23rd had little effect against a now strengthened defence, and the offensive died away. The exhausted troops were not relieved.

The following days produced ominous signs that the enemy was preparing a counter-stroke, but the Army Commander and the Corps Commander mainly concerned paid little heed to such warnings, and sug-

gestions for counter-measures were lightheartedly rejected. On the misty morning of November 30th, after
a short hurricane bombardment with gas and smoke
shell, the Germans thrust at both flanks of the new
salient made by the British advance. In the north it
was parried, but in the south it broke through. Disaster was narrowly averted, and the British had to
abandon a large part of their original gains.

An official court of enquiry was subsequently held:
following Byng's opinion, it placed the blame for the
costly surprise on the negligence of the troops—who,
in fact, had paid the price for the neglect of warnings
which they had given in vain. The sacrifice, however,
was not in vain, for their original attack had disclosed
the value of a new method and recalled the old value
of surprise. Nine months later the object-lesson would
bring forth unblemished offspring.

9. THE CAPTURE OF JERUSALEM

The bells of London had rung for the "victory" of
Cambrai. A week after their echoes had acquired
an ironical note there came the definite gain of a thou-
sand-year-old objective—Jerusalem. Because of the
gloom of the year, this December success had a moral
value far in excess of the material effect.

Lloyd George had been eager to retrieve Murray's
double failure in the spring, and casting round for a
suitable commander, had offered the post to Smuts.
But Smuts was deterred from accepting it by a broad
hint from Robertson that any attempt to make "a first-

class push in Palestine" would be obstructed by the
War Office. As Lloyd George continued to press for a
new and enterprising man, Robertson produced Allenby. The new commander went to Palestine with
the assurance of the Prime Minister's readiness to provide what he asked. Two further divisions were sent as
an instalment. Then early in October, he was told that
the Government wished him to advance to the Jeru-
salem-Jaffa line—what force would he need to reach
this objective? The message went through Robertson.
Allenby asked for a further thirteen divisions, more
than a quarter of a million men—having been given
an exaggerated estimate of the forces that the Turks
might be able to bring against him. Robertson
promptly seized on Allenby's vast demand to show the
impracticability of the whole scheme. Jellicoe reinforced Robertson's arguments by demonstrating the
shipping could not be provided for such a huge scale
of force.

But the plan was not to be thus baulked. At the end
of October Allenby attacked with the force he actually
had, and these gave him a superiority of nearly three
to one over the Turks available to oppose him. By the
use of subtle ruses, and by operating on a wide front,
these odds were multiplied at the crucial points. Beer-
sheba was seized as a first move, under cover of a feint
against Gaza; a week later Allenby broke through the
enemy's weakened centre. Although the cavalry pursuit failed to profit by the opportunity of cutting off
the enemy's forces, the Turkish retreat was steadily
followed up. By November 14th Jaffa was taken and

the main force wheeled to the right for an advance inland on Jerusalem. After suffering a check in the hills, Allenby spent a fortnight in preparation for a renewed attempt. This time he succeeded, and Jerusalem was occupied on December 9th.

1918

1. THE DAWN OF 1918

The events of 1917 had provided a fresh incentive to the movements for unity of direction among the Allies. In August Painlevé, prompted by Foch, had urged on the British Government the necessity of forming an Inter-Allied General Staff, suggesting Foch as its chief. Lloyd George was fully in accord with the principle, but doubtful whether British public opinion was ripe for it. Also, he was averse from an organ of an exclusively military nature. Early in September he sounded President Wilson on the idea of an "Allied Joint Council with permanent military and probably naval and economic staffs attached to work out plans for the Allies." He also consulted French and Henry Wilson, who strongly supported the idea.

The Caporetto disaster gave the scheme a fresh impulse. It was defined and put to the French, who promptly approved it. So did the Italians, at the conference held at Rapallo early in November. A Supreme War Council was now formed, composed of the principal statesmen of the different countries, together with permanent military representatives—originally Foch, Henry Wilson, and Cadorna. It is only too clear that the attitude of some of the soldiers towards the scheme varied according to its effect on their personal positions. Those whose influence it strengthened naturally supported it. Robertson, on the other hand, walked out of the conference as soon as the idea was mooted, saying: "I wash my hands of this business."

In the economic sphere, the establishment of the Council led to an early improvement in the combination of munition, shipping and food resources. But in the military sphere it became a bone of contention. Both the French and the Americans wanted to give the military committee executive powers, with a president who would virtually be Commander-in-Chief of the Allied Forces. But the British political and military chiefs were in accord, although from different motives, in standing out against this proposal when it was put forward in November. Lloyd George feared that it might weaken the already precarious control of the soldiers by their Governments; while Robertson and Haig feared that it might again give the French a deciding voice in the control of the British Army.

The problem was complicated by the fact that Pétain was simultaneously urging that the British ought to take over a larger share of the front. Haig had reluctantly met Pétain so far as to agree that he would extend his line a further twenty-five miles, southward to the Oise. Even so, the French with approximately a hundred divisions would hold 325 miles of front, while the British with sixty divisions of larger size would hold 125 miles. On a mileage basis the French were amply justified in their complaint, but the British pointed out that they had to cover the vital Channel ports, had less room to fall back, and had a higher proportion of the enemy already on their front. These were just reasons for holding a proportionately smaller front, but the question remained whether the actual proportion claimed was a fair one. To weigh such an involved question required an attitude of the purest scientific detachment, whereas it had to be resolved by men of determined ideas and strong national bias, who had difficulty in seeing the other side's point of view.

Another complicating factor was the slowness with which the men who had been conducting the offensive for so long adjusted themselves to the new problem of meeting a German offensive. In his October appreciation Haig had expressed the opinion that, even if Russia dropped out the most that the Germans could send to the West were a further thirty-two divisions (they actually sent fifty-two). But he viewed this possible reinforcement merely as a hindrance to the renewed Allied offensive. Not a word of his argument suggested the possibility that the Germans might take the offensive, even if reinforced. So little did he think of having to meet a German offensive that to those of his own staff who were concerned with the strengthening of defences he declared: "Your old back lines aren't going to be of any use." And it was on the score of his own projected offensive that he originally objected to taking over more frontage. But when Russia's collapse became unmistakable he abruptly veered round to a defensive outlook—and on this ground continued his objection to an extension of front.

As the danger became nearer the French became more insistent on a readjustment of shares, and Clemenceau, their new Prime Minister, insisted that Haig should take over fifty-five miles instead of a mere twenty-five miles. He threatened to resign unless his demand were met, but was persuaded to submit his case to the Versailles committee. Here a compromise was produced, by which the British were to take over half the distance in dispute. Thereupon Haig threatened to resign. While the Supreme War Council was still hugging its dilemma Pétain saved the situation by agreeing, in a personal talk with Haig, to the extension originally promised. The Supreme War Council swallowed its dignity and wisely accepted this private settlement.

The dispute, however, gave an impetus to the movement towards co-ordination. For it was felt that if the Allied Commanders-in-Chief had such difficulty in settling a mere question of frontages, there would be worse trouble in deciding upon combined action in emergency. So the advisory committee was developed into an executive board, with Foch as chairman, which should control an inter-allied general reserve of thirty divisions. Robertson was strongly in favour of such a reserve but wished it to be controlled by the Chiefs of the two national General Staffs, Foch and himself. Lloyd George objected to this, not only because it perpetuated the sectional tendency but because it would preserve Robertson's personal domination. When the executive board was formed, Robertson fought hard to secure a place on it instead of

Henry Wilson. His frustration led to a political storm in London. The Prime Minister, swinging round, appointed him to the Versailles post while proposing that Wilson should succeed him as Chief of the General Staff at home with reduced functions. Robertson refused, and the domestic crisis continued, the Cabinet being divided against itself. Then Robertson was offered his old post on the new terms. His rejection of them braced the Prime Minister to accept the challenge: Robertson was removed, and replaced by Wilson, while Rawlinson was sent to Versailles.

This reshuffle did not remove the main obstacle to the inter-allied reserve. When Haig was called on to contribute his share—nine divisions—he replied that he had made his dispositions to meet the coming offensive, had assigned all his divisions accordingly, and could spare none. Foch in desperation appealed to the Supreme War Council, but Haig had gained Clemenceau's support and Lloyd George hesitated to risk a fresh political crisis. Haig's refusal was a paralysing stroke to the Versailles board and the idea of an inter-allied reserve. He preferred to rely on a personal arrangment he had made with Pétain for mutual support, although this only provided for a reinforcement of six divisions, and even these were not expected to be available until the fifth day of an emergency.

In making his dispositions, Haig placed the bulk of his strength in the north. Three armies, the Third, First, and Second, covered the northerly two-thirds of his front from near Cambrai to the sea, with a total

of forty-six divisions. The Fifth Army covered the
remaining third to the Oise, part of it newly taken
over and in a poor state of defence, with only fourteen divisions available. In making this distribution
Haig was influenced by the importance of the Channel ports, and by the narrowness of the space which
separated them from the front in the north. He was
also strong near Arras, because he regarded this natural bastion as a key point, and thus military theory
suggested that the enemy ought to attack it. This firm
preconception seems to have led him to pay special
attention to all signs that the enemy were preparing
an attack there, and to discount the abundant warnings he received from the air and the Fifth Army of
an impending attack further south. This delusion per-
sisted until the eve of the German offensive, for as
late as March 16th the G.H.Q. conclusion was: "No
serious attack is to be expected south of the Bapaume-
Cambrai road."

2. THE MARCH BREAK-THROUGH

Disappointed of a result by the submarine campaign and determined not to forgo their dreams
of annexation by a negotiated peace, Hindenburg and
Ludendorff decided on a bid for victory by attack on
land. In this they were encouraged by recent events.
Having repulsed the British effort to capture the Belgian coast, the German military chiefs were no longer
ready to contemplate its evacuation as the price of
peace. On December 11th, 1917, Hindenburg wrote

to the Chancellor, "As our military situation has developed particularly favourably, I can no longer recognize the necessity for a partial renunciation of the military demands but must press them once more to their full extent." The Foreign Office representative at headquarters reported: "They are feeling very big here at present and full of the idea of smashing the enemy." The Supreme Command was supremely confident of final victory.

There was, however, more realism in their preliminary estimate of the situation than in Haig's—more care to take account of unfavourable factors. In contrast to the Allies, they insisted that the guiding principle must be to strike "where the enemy is *weak*" and that "all means must be applied to achieving the first essential of success, namely, surprise." In December Lieut.-Colonel Wetzell, the head of the Operations section, drew up an appreciation. He remarked that:

"Any prospect of success in the West depends upon other principles than those which hold good for the East or against Italy. We must be quite clear what these principles are before estimating what is attainable and taking into account, in the light of our previous experience in the west, human probabilities; otherwise we shall be led astray and select objectives which, in view of the character of our opponents, we are not likely to reach."

He then discussed the two main opponents. First, the British:

"The artillery, like the British tactics as a whole, is

rigid and stiff. The British infantry is very fully equipped with machine-guns, etc. We have a strategically clumsy, tactically rigid, but tough enemy in front of us.

"The French have shown us what they can do. They are just as skilful in the tactical use of their artillery as of their infantry. Their use of ground in the attack is just as good as in the defence. The French are better in the attack and more skilful in the defence, but are not such good stayers as the British. The British are tied strategically to Flanders; the French are free."

After considering the problem presented by the enemy's power of switching reserves laterally through "the excellent railway communications behind his front," he went on to describe the difficulties of obtaining a complete surprise in the light of recent examples.

"Further, it must not be forgotten that in a successful offensive, the attacker will be forced to cross a difficult and shot-to-pieces battle area and will get gradually further away from his railheads and depots, and that, having to bring forward his masses of artillery and ammunition columns, he will be compelled to make pauses which will give time to the defender to organize resistance."

This led him to utter a warning against conceiving "too optimistic hopes" of the rapidity of any breakthrough attack.

"We can only achieve a very great and decisive success by a skilful combination of a series of attacks carried out in close connection with each other."

As regards the prospects of different directions of attack, he considered that "the double attack to pinch out Verdun" promised the most decisive effect, since it would paralyse the French who were now the most dangerous opponent "because they are strategically free." If, however, the choice fell on an attack against the British, he preferred one in the general direction of Hazebrouck, but considered that it should come "as the last link."

"If we decide to attack the British—which promises success on account of their lack of strategical flexibility—in my opinion, we must set the whole British front tottering by a skilful combination of successive attacks definitely mutually connected with each other, on different sectors of the front and finally in the direction of Hazebrouck, making full use of railways for the rapid transfer of forces. In my opinion, we shall not achieve this purpose by a single attack at one spot, however carefully it is prepared. For this the British front is too narrow in relation to the available British forces."

To show the "correctness of this principle" he recalled the British attack at Cambrai, remarking "in what a difficult situation should we not have found ourselves if this blow had taken place simultaneously with the great Flanders attack!" He then declared that the Germans' "guiding thought . . . must be to put the British in this situation."

The original break-through might suitably be made on the St. Quentin sector, but the devastated area of the old battlefields was a potential check on rapid progress beyond a certain line. Hence, he proposed that the aim of the Cambrai-St. Quentin attack should be merely to draw the British reserves away from the Flanders front, and that it should pause short of the worst part of the devastated area, thrusting on the British the difficulty of forming a new front in the midst of this battle-scarred region. "About a fortnight later" should come the break-through attack towards Hazebrouck ("the scheme St. George"), "attacking the British in flank and in rear and thus set the whole British front tottering and then roll it up from the North."

It was fortunate for the British that Ludendorff departed from the plan designed by his strategic advisor. He accepted the idea of attempting his initial break-through on the Cambrai-St. Quentin sector, but was reluctant to break off his advance so early as Wetzell suggested. Moreover, the Arras bastion had a theoretical attraction for him as it had for Haig, and he extended his front of attack thither, massing a considerable part of his reserves at this spot where the British were strong, at the expense of the southern wing. The effort was a breach of his new principle, of taking the line of least resistance. It would also prove to be at the expense of the Hazebrouck attack, which was later in delivery, and weaker in force, than it should have been. Too much was staked on the first blow—because

Hindenburg and Ludendorff were inclined to assume that a second would not be needed.

In their means of achieving surprise and cracking the enemy's defences, they were also handicapped by their own lack of foresight. They had been even slower than the Allies to recognize the value of the tank: not until August, 1918, when it was used to strike them a deadly blow, did they place it in the "urgent" class of war material. General von Kuhl, Rupprecht's Chief of Staff, considered that the help of tanks would have made all the difference to the final issue, in the March offensive, "if six hundred tanks had paved the way for our infantry." He confessed that the fault lay with the military leaders—"our industries were capable of producing them."

For lack of such a master-key, Ludendorff had to depend on familiar means. But he forged a new technique from a compound of various elements—stealth of preparation, so that the assaulting divisions came up by night; masses of artillery which opened fire without disclosing their presence by previous "registration;" a brief but intense bombardment, largely of gas-shells; infiltration tactics by which the leading infantry acted as probing fingers while those who followed pushed in wherever the defence was weakening, instead of where it held firm; the different lines of reserves all beginning to move forward at zero hour. Colonel Bruchmüller was the designer of the new artillery tactics, Captain Geyer of the new infantry tactics.

Nature rewarded this research for surprise by providing the cloak of fog under cover of which the attacks broke into the British·position. The new German technique then sufficed to develop this opening into a break-through.

About 4-35 a.m. on March 21st the bombardment opened—there were over 6000 guns on the sixty-mile front. Six hours later, though in some sectors earlier, the German infantry began their infiltration. A thick fog covered the countryside. The British forward zone was quickly overrun, and by nightfall the battle zone had been breached in several places.

North of Flesquières a huge pocket had been made on the Third Army front, while the troops in the old salient itself, although not directly attacked, had suffered thousands of casualties from a gas bombardment. But "in spite of G.H.Q. warnings, the Third Army was not yet prepared to abandon the last tract of ground won in the Battle of Cambrai." Byng's reluctance to make a timely withdrawal endangered both his own front and his neighbour's. For the Fifth Army, the weaker, made a better resistance on most of its front, although south of St. Quentin, where its troops were very thin, it was driven right out of its battle-zone.

Next day there was again a fog. The pressure on the projecting centre of the Fifth Army became so severe that it fell back to the Somme—some ten miles behind. This river-line was forced on the 23rd, under cover of a fog. The British front now sagged badly, and had become disjointed as it was pushed back and back through open country. G.H.Q. was slow to send Gough any reserves and had even put a brake on his moving up the few he had. Gough had recorded that they "did not seem to grasp the seriousness of the situation . . . it was important that G.H.Q. should realize the position, stripped of all illusions, and I began to think that I had not succeeded in making G.H.Q. understand." His complaint of their curiously lighthearted attitude is confirmed by those who were at G.H.Q. at the time.

This confidence suffered a sudden collapse, hastened by events on the Third Army front. For here Byng's belated withdrawal from the Flesquières salient became disjointed, producing a state of confusion and depression which had far-reaching ill effects. It nullified the success of the reserves further north in stabilizing the line and largely contributed to the break which arose between the Fifth and Third Armies. The British Command, indeed, was led on the 23rd to contemplate falling back "north-westward—to cover the Channel Ports," thus abandoning touch with the French.

Pétain was quick to detect this inclination, already suggested by Haig's original dispositions, while Haig heard that the French reserves which were now arriving showed more signs of covering their own flank than of filling the chasm. The two Commanders-in-Chief met on the night of the 24th. Pétain complained to Haig: "You withdraw your hand in proportion as I'm stretching out mine towards you." He showed that his primary intention was "to keep the French Armies together as one solid whole," and warned Haig that if the British gave way further the French would "fall back south-westwards in order to cover Paris." This intimation was a shock to Haig, who expected the French to fill the breach.

Feeling that Pétain was more conscious of his responsibility for the French Army, than for the common front, Haig sought a means of overruling him, and telegraphed to London, asking Milner and Henry Wilson to come over at once with a view to the appointment of someone who would overrule Pétain. If Haig had opposed the idea of an Inter-Allied Chief when there was a risk of his reserves being taken away, the position was different when he needed French reserves. The change in his outlook was in accord with human nature.

The sequel was that at a conference at Doullens on the 26th Foch was appointed to "co-ordinate" the operations on the Western Front. In this hour of crisis, his determined air and confident promises went far to restore confidence behind the front, while the news that someone fresh had taken charge had a similar effect in the British fighting line. In reality his appointment made little difference to the flow of reinforcements. And although on April 14th he secured the title of Commander-in-Chief of the Allied Armies, it gave him no real power of command. As he confessed himself later: "I was no more than conductor of an orchestra . . . say, if you like that I beat time well." In Haig, Pershing, and Pétain he had to contend with three men of strong will, who would not brook intereference nor accede to his desires more than their own judgment allowed, fortified by the right of appeal to their own Governments. He could coax them, but not control them. Thus plans remained a compromise, sometimes with ill-effect. Still, as the fighting troops assumed that the united command was a reality, its effect on them was, and remained, real.

When the Doullens conference was held, and for some days after, the German tide was still flowing in. On the 27th it reached Montdidier, a penetration of nearly forty miles, cutting one of the railways between Amiens and Paris. But it made little further progress, and gradually died away.

In stemming the tide, the dogged resistance of countless small packets of British soldiers, often separated from any support as well as from the control of the higher command, was a definite factor. So was the arrival of French reserves. Although to the hardpressed British they seemed irritatingly slow to appear, thereby producing an unjust sense of grievance which has lasted long, it is a fact that Pétain far exceeded the promise on which Haig had counted. Instead of the mere six divisions of the original agreement, nine were on the scene by the fourth evening, and a further thirteen were on the way. And it was Wetzell's verdict that the main factor in frustrating the German aim was "that the French by skilful utilization of their railways, and, even more, owing to the unsuspected capacities of their motor transport and their motorized artillery units, succeeded at the last

moment in closing the breaches on the Somme, on
the Avre, and near Montdidier."

The Germans contributed at least as much to their
own frustration. From the Supreme Command down-
wards, the majority were unable to grasp the implica-
tions of their new tactics in adequate degree. As Wetzell remarked at the Reichstag enquiry: "It was just at
decisive points that individual corps and divisional
commanders had not the sense to free themselves from
the trammels and habits" of the past.

But Ludendorff himself failed to fulfil the new doctrine which he had promulgated. For he dissipated
too large a part of his reserves in trying to redeem tactical failures instead of exploiting the line of least
resistance. For several days he kept a brake on Hutier's
Army in the south where progress was easy, while trying to force the Arras bastion. As this did not yield
to leverage on its flank, he launched a direct assault
against it on the 28th. There was no mist to cloak it,
and the attack collapsed under the fire of the expec-
tant defence. Ludendorff then altered his direction—
but only towards a fresh obstacle. For he threw the
weight of his reserves into the central advance towards
Amiens across the 1916 battlefields, instead of backing
up Hutier. The old battlefields imposed the check
that Wetzell had foreseen, and the surge towards
Amiens soon subsided.

The Allied air attacks multiplied the difficulties of
supply. But in the days of supreme oportunity the
German advance had suffered even more from temporary excess of supply, due to the retreating enemy's

abandonment of their stores. Troops who had long suffered from want of food and many other needs, owing to the economic blockade, could not resist the temptation which the well-filled British depots, offered and turned aside to pillage. When they had recovered, the military opportunity was fading. They were left with the reflection that they had been deceived by comforting lies about the effect of the submarine campaign. The sight of these plentiful depots made them think that the enemy's resources were inexhaustible. That impression would deepen when their own attacks ceased to bear fruit, and would produce a growing sense of depression.

Ludendorff had taken 80,000 prisoners, and had crippled the Fifth Army, but he had missed the strategic decision on which he had staked so much. Moreover, by pressing his effort too long, when the difficulties began to exceed the prospects, he had drained his own resources to the detriment of a second blow.

The British, however, had suffered a shock which was all the greater because such an extended retreat had not entered the realm of calculation. The troops had been prepared for resistance in depth, but not for a retreat in the open. Nothing had been done to train them as a whole for a fighting withdrawal. To men who had so much experience of offensives which ended in shallow advances, it seemed hardly conceivable that a German attack should go much further than their own. This helps to explain the exhilaration with which the first news of the attack was greeted at G.H.Q.—the Germans, it was said, would now get a

dose of their own medicine. Even if they succeeded
in forcing the Fifth Army to give some ground, it was
a sector where there was plenty of room for the purpose. And the spectacle would be a lesson to the British Government to be more generous in meeting
G.H.Q.'s demands for reinforcements. After that lesson had taken effect, any ground that was given up
could be regained by a counter-offensive.

The atmosphere changed when the crisis developed.
And from it grew a controversy which for many years
obscured the causes of the breakdown, and hindered
a scientific examination of them. The result was generally attributed to the overwhelming strength of the
German attack, and as the Government was able to
scrape together large reinforcements to repair the
losses—140,000 were sent out as drafts—it was natural
that Haig should have seized on to this fact to shift
the responsibility on to the statesmen's shoulders,
ascribing his defeat to lack of troops. It is remarkable
how long that excuse has passed without analysis of
the facts. In a sense, of course, almost every defeat in
history is due to the loser being too weak. But serious
criticism demands a sense of proportion—and of possibilities. A commander in the field is naturally anxious to obtain as many men as he can. It is not within
the normal soldier's province to appreciate the manifold difficulties and ultimate dangers of levying fresh
taxes on the nation's man-power. That is for the Government to weigh.

The British strength had certainly been weakened,
materially as well as morally, by the prolonged drain

of Passchendaele. For that weakness, the responsibility falls on Haig, since he had pursued his offensive and incurred huge losses in disregard of his pledges to the Government. Nevertheless, if this experience might be held a fair excuse for the Government, they could not escape the ultimate responsibility if in fact Haig's defeat was due to insufficient numbers when more troops might have been sent. The crux of the controversy is whether the German break-through was due to the weakness of Haig's forces.

On analysis this does not appear to be true. The British forces were twenty per cent stronger as a whole, and only three per cent less in fighting troops at the beginning of 1918 than the year before, when they had to undertake the offensive—a much bigger undertaking. Before the German attack came they were reinforced by a further 167,000 fighting troops— equal to an additional fifteen per cent.

Moreover, the fact emerges that the Germans had no appreciable superiority in the total of men or guns over the Allies. Since the Germans had been able to resist the Allied attacks in 1917 despite a heavy inferiority, the statesmen were justified in assuming that the Allied armies as a whole could hold their own. And as the national Commanders-in-Chief annulled the scheme for an inter-allied reserves, preferring to make their own arrangements, the responsibility logically rests with them if one national sector proved unduly weak.

The question still remains whether the British sector was really too weak. The idea is not supported by

the facts. For the total strength that the Germans concentrated on the British front gave them only a three
to two superiority—smaller odds than the Germans
had faced in 1917. That they doubled this superiority
on the Fifth Army front was a matter of generalship—
Haig's sphere of responsibility. Granting the wisdom
of being stronger in the north, were the actual pro-
portions reasonable? The G.H.Q. records show that
Haig's dispositions were made and maintained in the
belief, in face of ample evidence, that the attack would
not fall on the Fifth Army. This shows that his distribution of strength was based on a false assumption
—that he underestimated the risk it involved, through
discrediting the warnings that came from the Fifth
Army and were confirmed by the air reports.

Even so, in the light of past experience, odds of
three to one are not sufficient to account for such a
break-through as the Germans achieved. But the odds
became greater in effect because of the new system of
defence by which the available troops were divided
between a Forward Zone and a Battle Zone, which
lay a mile or two behind. The system was copied from
the Germans, but its essential idea was changed. Instead of using the Forward Zone as a spring-buffer to
absorb the initial shock, the British command held it
in strength. The Official History states that no less
than a third of the British infantry were posted in the
Forward Zone, so being exposed to the full effect of
the enemy's bombardment. And when the attack came
"the Forward Zone as a whole was overrun at the first
rush," and its occupants overwhelmed. Thus about

a third of the British infantry strength was forfeited before the battle really began. Such a fact makes it impossible for any fair critic to ascribe the responsibility for any weakness that developed to the insufficiency of troops provided by the Government.

But scientific criticism must probe further to see if there were other conditions that contributed to the result. A vital one is apparent in the blanket fog. For in the words of the Official History: "Like the obscurity of night, it rendered nearly useless the machine-gun, that weapon which, given opportunity, can in a few moments destroy any balance of numbers with which an attack may start." The hazards inherent in the distribution, strategic and tactical, of the British forces might not have materialized but for the presence of fog. For that probability of the season the British defence schemes had made no provision.

If the combined effect of these factors be weighed, there is adequate explanation of the failure of the defence—it was essentially a technical failure arising from maladjustment to the actual conditions. It was human, but hardly honest, that those who were responsible should have tried to shift the blame onto other shoulders.

3. THE APRIL BREAK-THROUGH

When at last compelled to realize that his bid for victory at one blow had failed, Ludendorff reverted to Wetzell's original scheme and decided to launch the "St. George" attack towards the important railway junction of Hazebrouck. Most of his reserves, however, had been used in the first blow and were now occupied in holding the huge salient that he had driven into the Allied front near Amiens. Late to make up his mind, Ludendorff was too quick to act. At a conference on April 1st it was decided to launch the stroke on the 9th, although only eleven fresh divisions could be moved there in time, instead of the thirty-five intended—because of this the "St. George" attack was appropriately rechristened "Georgette." His belated haste led also to the sacrifice of concealment, thus jeopardizing the chances of surprise.

But fate was kind to Ludendorff—redeeming his chance by providing him with obtuse opponents, with an unexpectedly soft spot, and with another cloak of fog. From the first day of April onwards the British aircraft reported a general northward movement of the German reserves and artillery, by road and rail, to the La Bassée—Armentières sector opposite Hazebrouck. The Official Air History states that "The air reports of the next few days, supplemented by air photographs, made it clear that the German concentration was of the most formidable kind."

Yet Haig was unshakably convinced that the enemy's next attack would be "a converging attack on the Vimy Ridge." The Official Air History records that: "There was nothing in the air reports and air photographs up to the 9th of April to support the view, held by General Headquarters, that a converging attack on the Vimy Ridge was likely. On the contrary the air information showed that the German troops opposite Arras were being drawn upon to supply reinforcements for the north." As in March, Haig's misjudgment seems to have arisen from his fixed idea that to capture the Arras bastion, his own strongest point, was the theoretically correct aim for the enemy. Hence, crediting them with his own persistency at Passchendaele, he assumed that they would go on trying despite previous failure.

His misjudgment was shared by the Army Commander on the threatened sector, Horne—who was noted for his almost consistent agreement with his chief. Horne had rejected proposals from his subordinates for rearward preparations to meet the danger of a break-through towards Hazebrouck. A suggestion that the reserves should occupy the second line in readiness had also been rejected. More unfortunate still was a decision taken in regard to the Portuguese corps, which was known to be in a bad state of morale. Horne withdrew one of its divisions from the line on April 5th, but left the other to hold the whole corps sector for a few days longer. It was "relieved" by the Germans.

On the morning of the 9th, the front was wrapped in fog. Under cover of this nine divisions were launched against three on an eleven-mile front. The Portuguese were swept away, and the breach was rapidly widened, northwards. By the second night it was thirty miles broad, though only five miles deep. Lack of reserves hindered the Germans in exploiting their initial success, while their "difficulties of supply under the increasing air attacks" formed a further brake on their momentum.

Ludendorff had thought of this attack only as a diversion. He was now lured on to follow the gleam of victory. He sent more divisions, although still in a piece-meal way. But his intention of delivering a converging attack against the Ypres salient was forestalled by a step back which the British made, abandoning the ground they had purchased so dearly six months earlier. With intent to do honour to his old chief, General Harington has related how Plumer first rejected the suggestion of a withdrawal from Passchendaele, then reluctantly consented, then repented his decision in agreeing to "those heartrending orders" and "made another attempt to stop them." The revelation does more honour to Plumer's heart than to his head. For with the aid of the reserves thus released the German effort to carry the dominating height of Kemmel was repelled, and by the 18th the storm subsided. The Germans had penetrated ten miles deep, but were still five miles short of Hazebrouck.

Without the saving withdrawal from Passchendaele, the danger could hardly have been averted. For the French were slower to send help this time. The appointment of Foch as Allied Commander-in-Chief, in name at least, had relieved Pétain of the direct responsibility of helping his ally: and now, it is clear, he felt that the security of his own front must be his prime concern. Foch, for his part, was the more reluctant to send French reserves northwards because of a preconceived idea that the enemy's correct course was to continue their attack towards Amiens. A week passed before he was persuaded that the German attack was more than a strong feint to cloak a renewed advance on Amiens. On the 14th he declared complacently, "the battle in the north is over." But at last, on the 16th, he belatedly admitted the danger and allowed the use of two divisions and a cavalry corps. And after the German attack had subsided, he sent three more.

These arrived in time for a resumption of the German offensive on the 25th, but not in time to consolidate their defensive position. And they were thrown off Kemmel Hill. For a few hours a last opportunity of breaking through was offered to the Germans. But Ludendorff apprehensively intervened to check them from exploiting it. When it was too late, he sanctioned a fresh effort, which was delivered on the 29th, and failed in face of a now hardening resistance. Here, once again, he had violated two fundamental lessons of war experience—never to check momentum; never resume mere pushing. Having failed, chiefly through his own wavering of mind and will, to sever any vital artery, he was left to hold a second great bulge in the Allied front.

4. THE MAY BREAK-THROUGH

Foiled in his half-hearted aim, Ludendorff henceforth became obsessed with the idea of redeeming his lost opportunity, and of striking a final and decisive blow at the British in Flanders. But, having now drawn the French reserves thither as well as to the Somme, he saw that he must first draw them back again to their front. With this idea he decided to attempt a diversion on the French front.

With good judgment the German command chose a sector so strong naturally that it was weakly held— the Chemin-des-Dames ridge north of the Aisne. It was further calculated that, this being the sector nearest Paris, the French reserves would be drawn there more easily. Owing to the way Ludendorff had drained his resources, the stroke could not be delivered until May 27th, but it was hoped to follow it with the decisive blow in Flanders by the middle of June.

In preparing this offensive against the Chemin-des-Dames, the German technique reached its highest level. To conceal the assembly of the forces most elaborate precautions were taken. Every artillery wheel had wood-wool wired on to its tyre; every axle was wired with a leather covering; every horse's hoofs were muffled in rags; every chain, ring, shield, or ladder was wrapped in straw. On the railways and roads, no vehicles were allowed to have a distinguishing mark, and troops made no movement by day except in small packets; and if these were on the open road when hostile aircraft appeared they turned about, as if marching away from the front. The attacking divisions were brought up by nightly stages, hiding in woods by day.

Nature provided a double-reward for this care. For the difficult problem of bridging unnoticed the River

Ailette which ran through no-man's-land was eased by the croaking of the frogs which swarmed in that valley. To this noise-screen was added the greater help of a thick ground-mist on the morning of the assault.

At 1 a.m. on May 27th, the bombardment opened on a thirty-mile front, between Reims and Soissons. A total of 3700 guns were employed, working on a system devised by Bruchmüller that was aimed to produce the maximum confusion in the defence. At 3-40 a.m. the barrage moved on—it consisted of "a hurricane of gas-shells in front followed by a sheet of shrapnel paving the way for the infantry advance." A wave of fourteen German divisions struck five Allied divisions—or, rather, the dazed survivors. These were swiftly overwhelmed. The defenders had five more divisions in reserve, but the bulk of these were rashly pushed forward and engulfed in the advancing flood, which swept on to seize the unguarded bridges of the Aisne. By nightfall it had reached a second barrier-river, the Vesle—a penetration twelve miles deep.

This startling success had been much aided by the Allied Command. Haig had once again expected that the enemy's next blow would be aimed to capture the Arras bastion. Foch was inclined to agree that the British might again be the target, but was more concerned with his own offensive schemes, which had already been forestalled once. How little he anticipated the Chemin-des-Dames stroke is shown by the fact that to this very sector were sent—for a rest—five battle-worn British divisions in exchange for the French divisions sent to Flanders. It is remarkable, however, that the American Intelligence, studying the question in detachment from preconceived views, arrived by deductive reasoning at the conclusion that the next German offensive would be against the Chemin-des-Dames sector, between May 25th and 30th. This reasoning eventually made an impression on the French Intelligence, but, as at Verdun two years before, the Operations Branch disagreed. This time it had an excuse in the comforting assurances of the local Army Commander, Duchêne, which were supported by the fact that air reconnaissances failed to detect any signs of the German preparations.

Duchêne's greater responsibility is that, by his dispositions and his complacent intolerance of advice from subordinates, he played into the enemy's hand. He insisted on massing his infantry in the forward positions, thus ensuring that once the Germans had swallowed this helpless cannon-fodder, there would be practically no local reserves to check their onrush. Further, most of the headquarters, communication centres, ammunitions and supply depots, had been pushed forward into the strip north of the Aisne. South of the river no second line of defence had been prepared. If a German staff officer had guided Duchêne's hand it would hardly have been possible to make more effective arrangements for smoothing the attackers' path.

Two days before the blow fell, the British came to suspect it, but to their warning the French General Headquarters replied early on the 26th that "there is no indication that the enemy has made preparations which would enable him to attack the Chemin-des-Dames position to-morrow."

Almost simultaneously two Germans were taken prisoner and, under cross-examination, disclosed the whole plan. Duchêne held a conference to discuss what measures could be taken to meet it. Nothing adequate could be done in the time: the alternative was to fall back immediately behind the Aisne. But the generals could not bring themselves to abandon such hallowed ground. They decided to stay—and lost their troops as well as the ground. Apart from the dead and wounded, 50,000 prisoners were taken.

If this sacrifice imperiled France it ultimately became the Germans' undoing. Once again Ludendorff was first surprised, and then ensnared by the unforeseen measure of his own success. Intending only a diversion, he had limited the objective to the high ground south of the Vesle. On reaching that line early on the 28th, the Germans halted. The situation was too tempting; and Ludendorff decided to push on. During the pause, the wine-cellars of Champagne fought for France. The German soldiers, like their Chief, were unable to resist temptation. At Fismes, and elsewhere, there were "drunken soldiers lying all over the road." Progress became slow despite the slightness of the opposition. On the 30th, the German centre reached the Marne, fifteen miles beyond the Vesle, but the wings were bent back. And the French had forestalled an attempt to extend the frontage of attack west of Soissons—by a timely step back. Moreover, the delay had gained time for Pétain to rush reserves to the scene—sixteen divisions were sent in the first twenty-four hours. The first few were thrown in as they arrived, and thrown back by the German tide. But on June 1st Pétain issued orders that further reserves should dig in, before the tide reached them, and thus form a vast semicircular dam to check and confine its slackening flow. Ludendorff had also taken a new decision, of fateful consequence. He postponed his intended blow in Flanders, and concentrated his efforts on developing his success against the French. With this aim, he sought to expand the flanks of the new breach, and also mounted in haste an attack to break down the vast "buttress" which separated the Marne breach from the Somme breach.

The first intention was frustrated by the strength of Pétain's new dam; its failure was signalized by the appearance of the Americans in the battle-line, and by the counter-attack which their 2nd Division delivered at Château Thierry on the Marne. The second intention was foiled when the German attack against the Noyon-Montdidier sector on June 9th was quickly brought to a standstill. The haste of preparation had forfeited concealment, so that the French were ready to meet it, and the Germans attacked with bare equality of strength. That they had some initial success was due to the sentimental conservatism of the local French commanders, who evaded Pétain's orders for an elastically yielding defence, finding an excuse in Foch's latest *directive* which ordained "a foot-by-foot defence of the ground." This folly, however, was not carried far enough to endanger the resistance in rear.

With the failure of the attack, the scales of the war tilted definitely against the Germans. Pétain forsook his natural caution and remarked: "If we can hold on until the end of June, our situation will be excellent. In July we can resume the offensive; after that victory will be ours."

5. MIDSUMMER NIGHTMARE

The German offensive, for all its air of success, had achieved for the Allies what their own offensives of 1915, 1916, and 1917, had failed to bring in sight. For three years the French and British military chiefs had talked confidently of the early exhaustion of the German Army under the "attrition" of their attacks. Yet the annual intake of German recruits had much exceeded the permanent loss that was inflicted, which amounted during these three years to about one and a half million men. Although during his Passchendaele offensive Haig had reported that the end of the German resources was in sight, in March, 1918 the Germans' strength on the Western and Eastern Fronts amounted to over 4,600,000. The number of their divisions had now reached its peak—235. This was nearly twenty per cent more than the number of German divisions when the Franco-British offensive of 1917 opened. Moreover, the average field strength of battalions was over 800 men. The moral strength, too, had recovered from the strain of Passchendaele—to a much greater degree than that of the British. General von Kuhl had himself felt too much of the strain of the defence to minimize its effect, yet his evidence after the war was that "those who saw the freshness and cheerfulness of the troops who took part in the 1918 offensive must have preserved an unforgettable impression." War-weariness was for the time forgotten in the intoxication due to the promises of victory held out by the Higher Command.

When the German offensive came to an end, the average field strength of battalions had fallen to 600 odd. Worse still, the annual intake had been used up in filling up the ranks to this level, and divisions were now being broken up. From now on the strength would fall continuously, with ever-growing momentum. The decline in morale was no less sharp. It was authoritatively admitted that "The breakdown of the offensive which had been undertaken with every hope of victory had a very depressing effect on the spirit of the troops."

The effect was much worse because stomachs were empty. The Allied blockade had now tightened to a stranglehold. Food and all other necessities were dwindling. The rations issued to the German troops were insufficient, both in quantity and quality, to keep them in a healthy state. Sickness became rampant and many of the men in the ranks, if not sick enough to be taken to hospital, were not fit enough to fight. Their anguish was increased by pitiful letters from home, where conditions were even worse. They were brought to realize that by fighting on they were injuring, instead of protecting their families. By this hunger pressure, loyalty to family and loyalty to country were set in opposition, thus imposing a breaking strain on the will of the soldier—a will now weakened by his own bodily ills. It is a wonder that in such conditions the German soldiers fought on even as long as they did.

While the German strength was waning, that of the Allies was waxing. The American forces were now pouring into France in numbers that much exceeded even the great losses of the British and French in resisting the German offensive.

That reinforcement had been slower to arrive than the hard-pressed Allied nations had expected. For the delay there were several causes, beyond the original lack of preparation. The United States Government had lost little time in deciding to create an army of millions, and within three weeks of entering the war had adopted conscription. But, according to Pershing, the Commander of the Expeditionary Force, "it was, with some exceptions, practically six months before the training of our army was under way." He blames the delay on the building of cantonments to house the newly raised troops. But in the opinion of General Peyton March, who became Chief of Staff of the United States Army in 1918, there was a further needless delay in using these troops after their arrival in France. For this he blames Pershing's conventional outlook, saying that "the practical effect of the Pershing policy was that large bodies of American troops . . . who had had from four to six months training, often more, in camp in America . . . found the keen edge of their enthusiasm dulled by having to go over and over again drills and training which they had already undergone in America." As other instances of Pershing's military conservatism, he cites the awkwardly cumbrous size of the divisions, and the demands for cavalry—which March resisted because it threatened to upset the shipping programme and because: "I knew that Great Britain and France had each had for a long time, in rear of the lines, large bodies of cavalry in reserve, simply eating their heads off and serving no useful purpose." Pershing was a cavalryman.

The main plank of Pershing's policy was his determination to build up an all-American army independent of the Allies. For its equipment he could not be independent: he stated himself that even "up to the end of the war no guns of American manufacture" of the main types used "were fired in battle." Mortars were almost entirely obtained from the British, and tanks mainly from the French. But in the control of those forces he was determined to allow no partnership. There can be little doubt that his policy was justified in principle from a national point of view, and that, where action was not urgent, it was also in accord with practical wisdom. In his stand for national sentiment he was but following the example of the French and British commanders: the only question is whether he carried it further in a time of crisis, to the point where he imperilled the Allied cause as a whole. As his own memoirs show, he was the main and often the sole obstacle in the way of giving the Allied armies early reinforcement. President Wilson was willing to respond to their urgent appeals. So was General Bliss, the American military representative at the Supreme War Council. But Pershing stood firm, and even when he was forced to yield something on paper, he was quick to recover it in practice.

The desire of the Allies, which became more insistent as the strain grew heavier, was that American infantry and machine-gun units should be sent as soon as they were ready, without waiting until complete divisions could be organized and dispatched. Pershing feared that if he yielded on this point the Allies would be reluctant to release them when his own higher organization was ready. If there were grounds for that suspicion, it would seem that he under-estimated his own powers of extraction. For if any one commander got his own way at all times and with all people, that man was Pershing—by the light of his own memoirs.

When the storm broke over the Allied front on March 21st, there were 300,000 American troops in France, forming eight double-sized divisions. Of these, two were in the line, holding quiet sectors. On March 28th, during the crisis on the Somme, Pershing relaxed so far as to declare that the American troops were at Foch's disposal for use whenever required. It was an inspiring gesture—although in actual fact he did no more than he had already arranged with Pétain. This was to relieve two more French divisions, by one American. Two months passed before more than four American divisions were used to help in holding the line. On May 25th, coincidently with the third German offensive, the 1st Division struck the first American blow in a local attack at Cantigny, near Montdidier.

During those two months, the imminent danger of collapse spurred the French and British Governments to ceaseless efforts towards hastening the intervention of the American forces. On April 25th, Foch bluntly told Pershing that "the American Army may arrive to find the British pushed into the sea and the French driven back behind the Loire, while it tries in vain to organize on lost battlefields over the graves of Allied soldiers." Pershing declared he was willing to take the risk. Nothing could shake his objection to using American troops to fill the gaps in the Allied ranks. "I thought that the best and quickest way to help the Allies would be to build up an American Army." How it could be the "quickest" was an argument beyond understanding.

At an emergency conference at Abbéville early in May, Lloyd George, echoed by Clemenceau and Orlando, said to him: "Can't you see that the war will be lost unless we get this support?" But Pershing was unmoved. They continued to press the point—"whereupon I struck the table with my fist and said with the greatest possible emphasis, 'Gentlemen, I have thought this programme over very deliberately and will not be coerced.'" The war was not lost and Pershing was thus proved correct. But disaster was averted by a margin so narrow that the allied armies had to pay heavy excess costs in order to prove him correct.

There can be little question, however, that after the Germans had spent their strength in these three great offensives, the entry of America's forces was a major factor in enabling the depleted Franco-British forces to take advantage of the Germans' exhaustion. It thus proved decisive in the long run—so far as the ultimate offensive of the Allied armies contributed to the ultimate decision.

The problem of quickening the flow of the American troops to France was eased when Lloyd George at Abbéville promised to "scrape together" additional British shipping. Pershing agreed that preference might be given, although only for two months, to infantry and machine-gunners so far as they were carried in British ships—thus leaving him free to use American shipping for the transport of artillery and technical troops to complete his divisional organization. From this point of view he had achieved a bargain wholly advantageous to his plan of building a self-contained American army. The rate of arrivals now increased to 300,000 troops a month—a number equal to the total loss of the British in meeting the March and April attacks. By mid-July there were twenty-one complete American divisions in France. The British also, besides recuperating, had been able to reconstitute the ten divisions which had been temporarily broken up.

6. THE SECOND BATTLE OF THE MARNE

Ludendorff had thrown his weight so heavily, if belatedly, into the push towards Paris that more than a month passed before he was able to gather reserves for a further effort. Unable to see that the tide had turned, and unwilling to admit the deterioration of his troops, he still imagined himself delivering the oft-delayed final blow against the British. But his information showed "the enemy in Flanders still so strong that the German army could not attack there yet." So he postponed this blow once more until he had tried yet another diversion—this time by an attack on either side of Reims, to break down the eastern buttress of the Marne salient. A further reason for this decision was that the German troops in this salient precariously depended for their supplies on a single railway. His advisers warned him that he must either expand or withdraw. Ludendorff chose the offensive course.

But this time the sector was not a weak one, and there was no surprise. Prisoners taken by the French from July 5th onward disclosed the intention, which was amply confirmed by air photographs of the preparations. There was neither a fog nor a "fog of war." Moreover, the French had a surprise in store for the attackers. After a week's argument Pétain had persuaded the gallant Gouraud, the Army Commander east of Reims, to adopt a recoiling buffer method of defence—absorbing the initial impetus of the attack by a lightly held forward position and awaiting the spent attackers on a strong position in rear. When the German offensive was launched on July 15th, its sting was drawn. The French artillery caught the attackers before they left their trenches; the French machine-guns took further toll of them as they pressed through the forward position; the French artillery pulverized

them in the open when they ran against the main position, beyond the cover of their own artillery. The
attack east of Reims proved a costly failure.

West of Reims, along the Marne, the attack had
more success—because the French commanders here
insisted on holding their forward position strongly,
and the Germans, crossing the river under cover of
darkness and a smoke-screen, were able to throw the
defence into confusion. But the attack petered out on
the 16th, after threatening to under-cut the Reims
buttress.

The menace had at least partially upset the plans,
then maturing, for a French offensive. Ever since his
appointment to supreme charge Foch, characteristic-
ally, had been devising projects for taking the offensive himself, only to be thwarted each time. He had
now assembled an army under Mangin on the west
side of the Marne salient, for a stroke against the
Soissons "hinge." He had intended to launch this before the German attack. But Pétain preferred to let
the enemy strike first and then strike back at them
when tired and entangled. He gained his way but was
partially baulked of his purpose. Owing to the failure
of his subordinates west of Reims to adopt his elastic
defence method he had to use most of his reserves to
repair the consequences of their folly. He therefore
decided to postpone Mangin's attack for the moment.
But Foch, full of offensive ardour, overruled him and
released the stroke on the 18th.

The French on this occasion tried the "Cambrai
Key." Without any artillery preparation, several hun-

dred small tanks suddenly emerged from the woods. A thick early morning mist cloaked the advance and they quickly broke through the German line. The infantry followed. But after a bound of four miles on the first day, the attack came to a standstill short of the jugular vein of the salient—although it had a superiority of about four to one. The Allies had not acquired the ability to exploit a success, and Mangin's attempt to push through a cavalry corps proved as vain a hope as in the past. On the 20th the other armies round the salient joined in the offensive, but their converging pressure merely pushed the Germans back and was never in sight of cutting them off.

Nine American divisions took part in this push, but for all their keenness they lacked the experience and the technique necessary to overcome the German resistance. The French, by contrast, suffered from too much experience. Thus the Germans slipped out of the bag, with a loss of 25,000 prisoners, and established themselves on a straight and much shortened line along the Vesle. The danger had led Ludendorff to postpone his Flanders stroke, intended for the 20th, but he now felt able to order preparations to go forward. That dream was soon dissipated.

7. THE "BLACK DAY"

For on August 8th the "Cambrai Key" was used again, with even more striking effects. This time the nerve of the German troops broke. The repercussion shook the Supreme Command.

Foch, who had prophesied victory so often when the facts did not justify the illusion, had as yet no vision of the end. In a letter to Clemenceau he declared: "The decisive year of the conflict will be 1919." But having gained the initiative, he had no intention of letting it slip. On July 20th he had told Haig: "It is essential to grip onto the enemy and to attack him everywhere that one can do so advantageously." And in a memorandum on the 24th he drew the conclusion: "The Allied armies have reached the turning point of the road. . . . The moment has come to abandon the general defensive attitude forced upon us recently by numerical inferiority and to pass to the offensive."

For years the Allied commanders had persevered with a theory of the offensive under conditions that made it futile. Now the conditions had at last come to meet the theory. In this simple explanation can be epitomized the remaining months of the war. Nevertheless Foch had learnt from those four years hard experience one important lesson—that surprise was necessary. "Recent operations show that this is a condition indispensable to success." It is true that the lesson was engraved throughout the records of the previous three thousand years—but somehow Foch and his fellows had missed it.

To keep up the pressure on the enemy while the Allied reserves were accumulating, Foch arranged with Haig, Pétain and Pershing for a series of local offensives, aimed to free the lateral railway communications. He had suggested for the British an attack in

Flanders, but accepted Haig's preference for one to disengage Amiens.

Here preparations were already being made by Rawlinson, now commanding the Fourth Army again. They were to prove that the British had at last learnt the art, as well as the necessity, of surprise. The plan was a compound of many deceptive devices—thirteen divisions, over 2000 guns, and 456 tanks were smuggled into the area undetected. The main blow was to be delivered by the Australian and Canadian Corps: the former, already on the spot, extended its front to lull the enemy into a false sense of security; the latter was brought down from Arras and only moved in a few hours before the assault. Meantime, a special fraction had shown itself obviously in Flanders.

Fortune now, as on July 18th, lent the cloak of fog to the Allies. It was thickened by smoke-shell. Under cover of it the tanks overran the enemy's flimsy defences. The attacking infantry, who here had odds of over seven to one in their favour, overwhelmed the nerve-stricken defenders. The day's objective six to eight miles distant, was easily gained.

Next day little was done, and thereafter the attack came to a standstill; partly through being checked by the old battlefields; partly because the Germans were quicker in moving reserves to close the breach than the British in deepening it. The attack, being purely frontal, pushed the enemy back on their reinforcements and thus helped to consolidate their resistance. The Tank Corps Staff had originally suggested that the fast whippet tanks might be sent on independently through the gap, before it could be closed, but this was too unconventional for the Higher Command, and the whippet tanks were tied to the cavalry.

Nevertheless, the first shock had made a deep impression. After hearing Ludendorff's confession, the Kaiser said: "I see that we must strike a balance. We are at the end of our reserves. The war must be ended." In Ludendorff's ultimate verdict: "August 8th was the black day of the German Army in the history of the war. . . . It put the decline of our fighting power beyond all doubt." Hot on the heels of defeat, he declared that peace negotiations ought to be opened before the situation became worse—but once again was too slow to realize how fast the tide was ebbing. Remembering how the strategic withdrawal of 1917 had dislocated the Allies' offensive, some of the more practical German leaders wished to repeat it now. But Ludendorff could not bring himself to take the risk with troops who had been fed on promises of victory.

8. THE EBBING TIDE

Foch, also, was slow to realize that his opportunity had passed. He urged Haig to push hard—but Haig now showed an awareness of the folly of hammering at hardening resistance. He had visited the front and seen the situation for himself. (It is worth remark that, in contrast to earlier years, officers at G. H. Q. adopted the practice in 1918 of seeing the ground for themselves before ordering attacks.) From Haig's objection to continuing pressure along the line of hardening resistance a new method developed a truer economy of force. Foch had already arranged that the offensive should be extended to neighbouring sectors, and Haig now contended that this indirect leverage was the better way to loosen the resistance. Foch gave way. On August 10th the French Third Army had struck on the south flank: on the 17th the Tenth Army, still further south: on the 21st, the British Third Army attacked to the north of the Fourth: on the 26th the First Army, beyond it, chimed in the strategic "tattoo." This widely menacing series of advances induced Ludendorff to sanction a general withdrawal to the old Hindenburg line, as far south as Soissons—thus abandoning almost all the ground he had gained at such a ruinous cost. By early September the withdrawal was complete. The British had collected over 70,000 prisoners in the three weeks' tattoo, and the French some 25,000.

On September 12th the last of Foch's original series of local offensives was completed, when Pershing erased the St. Mihiel salient on the far side of Verdun. This stroke did not come as a surprise to the Germans, who had been meditating a withdrawal. But they hesitated too long over their decision, and although they began it in the night before the attack was launched they were overtaken and badly hustled by the swiftness of the American onrush, losing 15,000 prisoners before they reached the shelter of the Michel line across the base of the salient. The bag would have been bigger if the plan had not put a check on the advance. It was an exhilarating result for the first performance of an independent American Army, but to many Americans it would leave the sore feeling of a missed opportunity.

For Pershing's original intention had been to exploit the expected opening success by pushing on, past Metz, towards the Germans' main lateral railway which there ran only twenty miles behind the Michel Line. This would have endangered the whole German position on the Western Front—if it could have been achieved. General Liggett, who played the chief part in the St. Mihiel stroke, and was an unusual realist, declared later that the possibility existed "only on the supposition that our army was a well-oiled, fully coordinated machine, which it was not as yet." But Pershing would remain sure that he had forgone a great opportunity—and would feel it the more because he had for once yielded to others' wishes. Foch had originally agreed to the bigger design. But on August 27th he received a letter from Haig which helped to change his mind. Haig had come to feel that the ending of the war in 1918 was both a possibility and a necessity. The unmistakable evidence of the enemy's decline gave him such slight encouragement as he needed to risk an assault on the Hindenburg Line, the strongest artificial defences on the whole Western Front. To reduce the risk he urged Foch to switch the main American attack from a divergent to a convergent direction. Each attack would thus, he calculated, assist the other.

Foch was the more receptive to the idea, because, stimulated by repeated success, he was already growing impatient with the new method of alternating attacks, each quickly broken off, which he had come to adopt. He was filled with the vision of a decisive victory by a simultaneous general offensive in which the British and American pincers should close on, and cut off, the main German armies. So he proposed to Pershing that the St. Mihiel attack should be limited to a mere excision of this salient, and that the main American attack should then be delivered in a northwesterly, instead of a northerly, direction. He further proposed that, to reduce the difficulties, Pershing's Army should attack west of the Argonne, while a mixed French and American army under a French commander should attack over the more difficult ground between the Argonne Forest and the Meuse. This led to a violent argument. Pershing declared: "Marshal Foch, you may insist all you please, but I decline absolutely to agree to your plan. While our army will fight wherever you may decide, it will not fight except as an independent American army."

The upshot was that Pershing gave up his own strategic plan for a share in Foch's, while Foch yielded to Pershing's declaration of independence. It was decided that the American forces would fight as a separate whole, free from any French control or advice. And Pershing chose the more difficult sector east of the Argonne. He made his task still harder, and America's cost greater, by rejecting Foch's suggestion that he might give up the St. Mihiel attack. The consequence was that he had not time to switch divisions

from one battlefield to the other, and had to use raw
divisions for the greater effort.

9. FOCH'S GRAND OFFENSIVE

"Everyone is to attack (Belgians, British, French
and Americans) as soon as they can, as strong
as they can, for as long as they can." That was the simple message in which Foch defined his intentions. But
in detail his grand offensive showed more design.

The great salient formed by the German front in
France between Verdun and Ypres was to be crushed
between a giant pair of pincers. The right pincer was
to be formed by the American army in the Meuse-
Argonne sector. It would strike first, on September
26th, and thus might draw off some of the forces facing the left pincer on the Cambrai—St. Quentin sector, where the defences were strongest and the enemy
most heavily massed. This pincer was formed by the
First, Third and Fourth British Armies. Each pincer
would be supported—if in the event not too energetic-
ally—by the French armies on their inner flanks. As a
supplementary lever a combined Anglo-Belgian force
was to make a forked stroke from Ypres on the 28th.

The American pincer appeared to have the greater
promise, not merely because the opposition was weaker but because the thrust was closer to the German
armies' line of supply and retreat, starting from a
point only thirty miles distant from the eastern end of
the main lateral railway. The British pincer, if it

could be thrust in deep enough, would threaten the other end of the railway and the line of retreat through the Liége corridor.

Pershing had no small ambitions. His untried troops were expected to break through the enemy's three successive positions in the first day, an advance of nearly ten miles; then exploit the success during the night and by the next morning be half-way to Sedan and the lateral railway.

After three hours intense bombardment by 2700 guns the American attack was launched on a twenty-mile front with odds of about ten to one. The Germans damped the shock by adopting the spring-buffer method of defence, with the main resistance some miles in the rear. The unexpectant Americans ran into this cunningly woven belt of fire when their initial impetus had been lost. Inexperience handicapped the attacking troops, and Pershing's orders ignored the experience which his Allies had bought so dearly in the past—tying the wings, which pushed past the flanks of the Montfaucon height, to the pace of the centre, which was held up. Checked by this self-applied brake, the attack could not regain momentum and the enemy had time to bring up reinforcements. Congestion and confusion on the roads behind helped to retard the advance.

Repeated efforts made small progress and at last in mid-October Pershing was forced to admit the stalemate, suspending operations in order to reorganize his tattered forces. He had covered only a third of the distance to the railway, and although some 18,000 prisoners had been captured, the cost to the Americans was over a hundred thousand casualties. In addition, according to General Liggett, the number of stragglers was "estimated as high as 100,000"—evidence of the widespread state of depression and confusion. This was not surprising when due account is taken of the risks of launching an untried force into a great offensive: the British at Suvla and Loos, the Australians at Anzac, had suffered the same sort of thing on a small scale. Here, a whole army, newly manufactured, suffered the strain—not merely a few divisions.

The left pincer proved more effective, though it stopped a long way short of being decisive—in a physical sense. In the misty dawn of September 27th, Byng's left and Horne's right assaulted the Canal du Nord. Penetrating on a narrow sector, the attackers spread out fanwise, and thus exerted a leverage which broke down the sides of the breach. Next evening they reached the outskirts of Cambrai. This advance brought them past the northern edge of the Hindenburg Line, and so formed a leverage on that line.

Meantime, on Rawlinson's front 1600 guns had been smothering the defences for fifty-six hours—the first eight hours with a new type of mustard-gas shell. Thus the defenders were driven to take refuge in their deepest shelters. Rawlinson's assault was to be launched on a nine-mile front, one British (the 46th) and two American divisions (the 27th and 30th) forming its spearhead. The prospect seemed more favourable to the American divisions, for whereas the 46th on the right was faced by the deep chasm of the St.

Quentin Canal, along the American front this canal passed through a tunnel. But the prospect was marred by a mishap: the 27th American Division had made a preliminary attack to clear three enemy advanced posts, and reported success. Then a doubt arose whether the posts were occupied by American parties or were still in German hands. The ill-consequence was that, on the 29th, the artillery put down the barrage half a mile in front of the infantry starting line. And in this fatal interval lay the posts, still with their German garrisons. The morning mist temporarily obscured them, but the American infantry had not been taught to regard it as a friendly cloak. Waiting, many of them were caught as it cleared, and were mown down in swathes. The collapse of their advance reacted on that of the 30th Division. Nevertheless, its men reached and breached the forward edge of the Hindenburg Line. But in their ardour they pushed on, and were taken in the rear by Germans who emerged from dugouts. Thus the effort of the Australians was spent in breaking down afresh this intervening obstruction, instead of in exploiting the original breakthrough.

The day was redeemed by the success of the 46th Division. Cloaked by the mist, which was much thickened by smoke, its men had gained the canal and swarmed across it before the Germans realized the situation. Another division then leap-frogged them and carried the advance beyond the rear edge of the Hindenburg Line. The driving in of this deep wedge created a new leverage which helped the renewed Australian attack in widening the breach.

By October 5th, the British had driven their way through the German defence system into open country, and had taken 36,000 prisoners. Mist, smoke, and the method of leverage had been three of the chief factors in their success, which was also helped by the fact that the attack, in contrast to that in the Meuse-Argonne, had opened with the assailants close to the main barrier.

The sequel proved a disappointment. The passing of the Hindenburg Line brought no marked acceleration of the advance, no sudden flooding of the open country beyond. Thirty miles still separated the British from the western end of the lateral railway. The British progress was not sufficiently fast or dangerous to produce any general, or even local, collapse of the German front. One cause was the wide area of reconquered and devastated country over which the British had now to haul their supplies. Another was that they had largely spent their force in breaking the Hindenburg Line—another 140,000 men had been lost in the past month's fighting. And the strategic failure of the Meuse-Argonne attack deprived Foch of a counter-attraction which might have been drawn off enemy reserves from the Cambrai front, easing the path of his left wing at this promising moment. But numbers were not as big an obstacle as a small machine—when this was handled by a stout-hearted man. Large numbers of the enemy, indeed, were now surrendering

freely. But not the machine-gunners. They had a
weapon which could riddle numbers, and strategic
calculations based on numbers. Like Foch and Pershing, Haig—who had hoped "to be in Valenciennes in
a few days"—was baulked once again by the delaying
power inherent in even a thin chain of machine-guns.

In Flanders another familiar obstacle had provided
a fresh proof of its powers. There the attack had also
broken through and swept forward eight miles in two
days, capturing 10,000 prisoners. But although the
Germans' resistance was not comparable with that of
Passchendaele, the attacking troops were then held up
because their transport could not get through the
mud. The offensive had to be suspended for a fortnight until the roads in rear were made passable.

10. THE FATAL STROKE

Unknown to Foch his offensive had proved more
deadly in anticipation than in fulfilment. Its
potential menace had made a decisive impression on
Ludendorff's military mind by coming at a moment
when he was shaken by the news of an indirect stroke
in a far-distant quarter.

Ten days before the grand offensive in France, a
crack had opened in the Balkans which had "sealed
the fate of the Quadruple Alliance." Such at least was
Ludendorff's judgment—and on his judgment at the
time hung that fate. He had hoped to hold fast in his
strong lines in France, withdrawing gradually to fresh
lines if necessary, while the obedient German states-

men were negotiating a favourable peace. But on September 15th the Allied Army in Salonika struck at the
Bulgarian front, using a spearhead of Serbs skilled in
mountain-war against a sector which was weakly held
because it seemed so strong by nature. Back in June
the Commander-in-chief there, General Guillaumat,
had been called back to France as a possible successor
to Foch or Pétain, then both under the cloud of the
Chemin-des-Dames collapse. When they were saved
by Clemenceau's support, Guillaumat was left in the
comparative inactivity of the military governorship of
Paris. Like Galliéni in 1914, he used it to vital purpose—by seeking to win permission for an offensive
at Salonika. Although the British commander at Salonika, General Milne, considered that the Bulgarians
were ripe for collapse, the British military advisers
both at Versailles and in London opposed the idea, declaring that success was not possible. Henry Wilson,
now in Robertson's shoes, donned Robertson's old
spectacles. Early in September Guillaumat came over
to London to plead his case. He convinced Lloyd
George, and consent was won.

Preparations had been going forward in Salonika
under Guillaumat's successor, Franchet d'Esperey.
The attack was launched on September 15th: in two
days the Serbs had penetrated twenty miles deep. The
whole of the enemy's front west of the Vardar collapsed under the converging pressure of the Serbs and
French, whose pursuit drove on towards Uskub. East
of the Vardar the British attack, on the Doiran sector,
was a failure but it at least helped to pin the enemy's

reserves. And when the withdrawal became general, the British aircraft, catching the retreating Bulgarians in the Kosturino Pass, turned it into a disorderly flight. With their army now split in two, the war-weary Bulgarians sought an armistice. Signed on September 29th, it severed the first root of the Quadruple Alliance and threatened danger to Austria.

That same day came the blow on the Hindenburg Line. The early reports were so disquieting as to offset the momentarily reassuring news from the Meuse-Argonne. After wrestling with his problems for some hours, Ludendorff broke down. That evening he took the precipitate decision to appeal for an armistice, saying that the collapse of the Bulgarian front had upset all his dispositions: "troops destined for the Western Front had had to be despatched there." This had "fundamentally changed the situations in view of the attacks then being launched on the Western Front," for although these "had so far been beaten off, their continuance must be counted on." Ludendorff had lost his nerve—only for a matter of days, but that was sufficient.

At this crisis Prince Max of Baden was summoned to be Chancellor, and to use his pacific reputation as a pledge of honour in negotiating peace. To bargain effectively and without open confession of defeat he asked and needed a breathing space of "ten, eight, even four days before I have to appeal to the enemy." But Hindenburg insisted that "a peace offer to our enemies be issued at once," while Ludendorff plaintively reiterated, "I want to save my army."

Hence on October 3rd the appeal for an immediate armistice went out to President Wilson. It was a confession to the world—and to the German people themselves—of defeat.

Within a few days the German command became more cheerful, even optimistic, when it saw that the breach of the Hindenburgh Line had not been followed by a break in the human fighting line. More encouragement came from reports of a slackening in the Allied pressure. Ludendorff still wanted an armistice, but only to rest his troops as a prelude to further resistance and to ensure a secure withdrawal to a shortened defensive line on the frontier. By October 17th he even felt he could ensure this without a rest. But his first impression, and depressions, had now spread throughout Germany as the ripples spread when a pebble has been dropped in a pool.

Bad news now came like gusts of wind—so that the ripples grew into waves, crumbling the will to resist.

11. THE COLLAPSE OF TURKEY

In the spring of 1918 Allenby's projects for a renewal of the offensive in Palestine had been upset by the breakdown in France, and the consequent recall of a large part of his British troops—replaced by Indian reinforcements. Twice, an attempted advance eastwards across the Jordan had proved a fiasco—with only the compensation that they persuaded the enemy commander-in-chief, Liman von Sanders, that the British, according to their custom, would try again in the same direction. While Allenby was reorganizing his forces, and improving their potential mobility, the Arabs continued to spread their raids along the Hejaz railway, drawing the enemy's attention still more to the inland flank. The late summer saw the maturing of Allenby's plans for a new offensive. Liman von Sanders anticipated this, and thought of frustrating it by a timely withdrawal. "I gave up the idea because we would have had to relinquish the Hejaz railway . . . and because we could no longer have stopped the progress of the Arab insurrection in rear of our army." Nearly half the Turkish forces were kept away from the British front by the elusive threats of a few thousand Arabs, directed by Lawrence.

During the month before Allenby struck, Lawrence wove a web of feints and fictions to convince Liman von Sanders that the British were going to come over the Jordan again. During the final three days of preparation, the Arabs cut the railways radiating from Deraa, the focal point of the enemy's communications. Helped by this distraction as well as by his own string of ruses, Allenby, from his army of quarter of a million men, was able to concentrate odds of about ten to one on a chosen sector near the Mediterranean coast.

On September 19th the infantry attack here opened like a door on its hinges, sweeping the dazed defenders aside. Through the open doorway the cavalry passed, and rode straight up the coastal corridor for thirty miles before swinging inland to close the bolt-holes in the enemy's rear. The only formed remnant of the Turkish forces tried to escape over the Jordan, but was caught in a gorge and bombed into chaos by the British aircraft. The wreckage of two "armies" was then rounded up by the cavalry. Another "army" remained, east of the Jordan, but a broken railway and the Arabs lay along its line of retreat. Its fate was a rapid attrition under incessant pin-pricks. The cavalry and the Arabs engaged in a race for Damascus, which was occupied on October 1st. They then continued to Aleppo and the junction of the Baghdad railway—completing a pursuit of 350 miles in thirty-eight days. Altogether some 75,000 prisoners had been taken at a cost of less than 5,000 casualties.

On October 31st, two days after the last bound was achieved, Turkey capitulated. Stripped of her forces in Syria and Mesopotamia, her capital was exposed to an imminent advance from Salonika.

12. THE COLLAPSE OF AUSTRIA

The Italian front had been comparatively quiet during 1918 save for a brief midsummer storm. After successfully resisting the enemy's attempts at the end of 1917 to force his new line on the Piave, Diaz had devoted himself to the overhaul of his forces, determined to abstain from offensives until the chances were completely favourable. When the crisis developed in France, he arranged to send an army corps thither as a token of goodwill and in compensation for the French and British forces retained in Italy. But he was reluctant to embark on any offensive diversion and found good reason for waiting in the signs that the Austrians were meditating an attack on his line. This came in June and took the form of a converging double thrust—down from the Trentino and straight across the Piave. The former quickly collapsed, the nerve of the war-weary Austrians breaking under the storm of fire that greeted them. The latter succeeded in crossing the Piave—"greatly assisted by mist and the smoke-screen." But reserves were rushed to the breach by motor, and hemmed in the attackers who, with the river rising in their rear and their spirits falling, withdrew in disorder a week later. The loss of over 100,000 men in this vain offensive bankrupted Austria's military power.

Diaz, however, was not to be hurried in following up his success—and resisted all pressure from his Allies to take the offensive until his chances were amply insured. Not until mid-October, after Germany's urgent appeal for peace, did he decide to move. But the plan was prepared. On October 24th, the anniversary of Caporetto, the Italian offensive opened with an attack in the Grappa region: this failed at heavy cost, although it helped to attract the enemy's reserves. And the flooding of the Piave led Diaz to suspend the attempt of the Eighth and Twelfth Armies to force the passage of the river. Further down the river in the sector of the mixed Tenth Army under Lord Cavan, a couple of British battalions had been ferried across by Italian boatmen to an island in midstream, under cover of night and a thick mist. Two nights later the capture of this island was completed by a British and an Italian division, and during the following day a thick fog covered the building of bridges. The two other divisions of Cavan's Army were brought over, and on the 27th a footing was gained on the far side of the Piave. In the other army sectors attempts to bridge the river had failed, but the reserves were now diverted to back up the successful crossing. Menaced by this spearhead, and with their troops already mutinying, the Austrian Army Command ordered a general retreat early on the 28th. The Italian advance now became general. Next day, with her forces splitting in two and her troops degenerating into a fugitive rabble, Austria begged for an armistice. It was granted on November 4th, after the Italians had drunk their fill of victory to drown the memories of Caporetto.

13. THE COLLAPSE OF GERMANY

That same day revolution broke out in Germany. It spread rapidly over a country that was soaked in a sense of hopelessness, its flames fanned by a hot wind of popular indignation against the leaders who had hidden the truth all too successfully. The memory of falsified promises was so strong and bitter that any further appeal for trust was foredoomed. Ludendorff had already been forced to resign. The Kaiser only added fuel to the flames by his reluctance to abdicate. The fleet mutinied when its leaders tried to send it out on a death-or-glory ride against the British fleet. On November 6th the German delegates left Berlin to treat for an armistice.

The Allied leaders had been debating for a month what they should demand before agreeing to suspend their advance. President Wilson declared that, in order to preserve the existing military superiority, the conditions must be left to the military advisers. This gave Foch a chance to make the military terms serve his country's political aims. He shrewdly remarked to Clemenceau that "the Armistice should give us full guarantees for obtaining the terms that we wish in the peace negotiations . . . for it is certain that only the sacrifices of territory agreed to by the enemy at the time of signing the Armistice will remain final." Foch declared: "You must strike while the iron is hot. If France intends to separate the Rhineland from Prussia, there is no time to be lost in shaping the Armistice accordingly." When Clemenceau rebuked him for intruding into the political sphere, Foch sought the support of President Poincaré, to reinforce his claim. And he took care to insert the occupation of the Rhine bridges in his draft terms. In addition, the enemy must surrender a third of their guns, half their machine-guns, and a large part of their railway material.

Pershing agreed that the terms would suffice to render Germany helpless, but protested against granting any armistice. It was a natural attitude in a keen soldier, for although he had built his army he had not yet consummated its achievement on the battlefield.

Haig, however, considered the terms too drastic—"The victorious Allied armies are extenuated. The units need to be reorganized. Germany is not broken in a military sense. During the last weeks her armies have withdrawn fighting and in excellent order. If it is really desired to conclude an armistice it is neces· sary to grant Germany conditions she can accept."

But to Foch no peace was of value without the Rhine, and he would not listen to Haig's objections. When the draft terms were discussed by the statesmen on November 1st, Foch admitted that the Germans were able to withdraw to a new and shorter line, and that the Allied armies were incapable of preventing this. But "the collapse of Austria, Bulgaria, and Tur- key" was bound to have an important effect on their situation, so that even if they rejected the terms now the end could only be postponed. The risk of this re- fusal was less than the risk of imposing milder terms.

If the conditions proposed by Foch went beyond the reality of the situation at the time they were framed, the situation was fast moving to meet them, although not on the Western Front.

The British armies, it is true, were still pushing on. By the time of the armistice they had reached Mons, the place where the little Expeditionary Force of 1914 had fought its first battle. And they had raised their bag of prisoners since September 26th to 88,000. But the Germans were now slipping away faster than they could be followed, and the British were obliged to pause while the communications across the de- vastated area were being repaired.

The American advance had been resumed on No- vember 1st, and because of its direction was potential- ly more dangerous. The number of American troops in France had now risen to two million, and in mid-

October Pershing had formed a Second Army under Bullard from the inactive forces east of the Meuse, handing over the First to Liggett, who thus took executive charge in the Meuse-Argonne. The fortnight's pause was well spent on reorganization, for the new advance went forward rapidly and smoothly in comparison with the past, reaching Sedan and the railway within a week. A further 8000 prisoners were taken, making a total of 26,000 since September 26th.[1] But the advance was too late to be a serious threat to the German withdrawal, and any large prospect here depended on whether the Americans, wheeling eastward, could force the new line which lay ahead and carry their advance a long stage further—towards the Saar.

A speedier prospect was offered by a newly prepared offensive against the untouched front in Lorraine, beyond Metz. For this Foch had assembled a Franco-American army, and the stroke was intended for delivery on November 14th. But Foch had learnt, at last, not to expect decisive results from any single stroke, and in retrospect he remarked that: "Its importance has always been exaggerated. It is regarded as the irresistible blow that was to fall and administer the knock-out to the Boches. That's nonsense." He had more hopes now of the effect of an advance on Germany's back door, for which three armies were to be brought

[1] Over the whole period of the Allied offensive campaign from July 18th to November 11th the captures were:

British Army	..	..	188,700 prisoners	2840	guns
French Army	..	..	139,000 "	1880	"
American Army	..	..	48,800 "	1424	"
Belgian Army	..	..	14,500 "	474	"

through Austria and across the Bavarian frontier. But as the Allied armies in the West were running to a standstill, the revolution in Germany was gathering momentum. The ever-tightening pressure of the blockade and the violent recoil caused by unexpected contact with hard facts were the irresistible forces behind it. Sudden exposure to truth is paralysing to those who have been guarded against it—and deadly to those who cover it up. The shock broke up organization, and checked any chance of reorganization on a new basis. With revolution in their streets, starvation in their homes, and disillusionment in their hearts, the Germans had become incapable of further resistance.

At 5 a.m. on November 11th the German delegates accepted the terms dictated to them in Foch's railway carriage in the Forest of Compiègne. Six hours later the last shots were fired. Thus at the eleventh hour of the eleventh day of the eleventh month of 1918 the war was brought to an end—symbolically suggesting that Western Civilization had been given a last chance to profit by experience, and to disprove Heine's saying: "We learn from history that we do not learn from history."

INDEX

INDEX

SPECIAL FACTORS

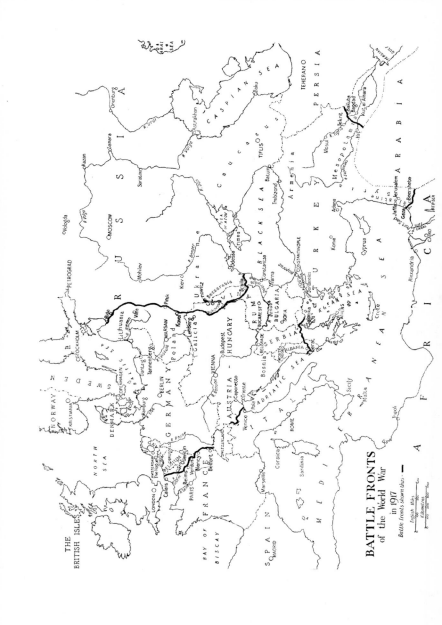

BATTLE FRONTS
of the World War
in 1917

Battle fronts shown thus: ▬

English Miles
0   100   200   300

Kilometres
0   100 200 300 400 500